Simply Soft Furnishings

Simply Soft Furnishings

**Better Homes and Gardens®
Creative Collection™**

Director, Editorial Administration
Michael L. Maine

Editor-in-Chief
Beverly Rivers

Editorial Manager	Art Director	Managing Editor
Ann Blevins	Brenda Drake Lesch	Karman Wittry Hotchkiss

Editorial Mgr., Custom Publishing	Debra E. Garner
Copy Chief	Mary Heaton
Editorial Assistant	Lori Eggers
Contributing Graphic Designer	Tracy S. Devenney
Contributing Illustrators	Glenda Aldrich, Barbara Gordon, Chris Neubauer
Contributing Editor	Shelley Stewart
Contributing Copy Editor	Pegi Bevins
Contributing Proofreaders	Angie Ingle, Joleen Ross, Marcia Teter

Vice President, Publishing Director
William R. Reed

Group Publisher	Maureen Ruth
Senior Marketing Manager	Suzy Johnson

CORPORATION

Chairman and CEO
William T. Kerr

In Memoriam - E. T. Meredith III
(1933 - 2003)

Publishing Group President
Stephen M. Lacy
Magazine Group President
Jerry Kaplan

simply
Living
Rooms

Plump up the pillows, smooth the slipcovers, and open the windows to transform your room into the inviting space you've always wanted.

Cottage Style

Pristine in White A formerly dark, craftsman-style house gets a fresh update with light-colored walls and trim and comfortably casual furniture. Solid or tone-on-tone white slipcovers contribute to the airy feeling in the room, while flawlessly unifying mismatched furniture. As long as the basic structure of the cushions is sound, versatile slipcovers disguise minor flaws such as stains on the fabric or scratches on the wood.
Best of all, washable cotton- or cotton/blend-fabric slipcovers are easy to launder, an important consideration if there are children or pets in the household. Notice the two types of slipcovers in this room. The made-to-measure cover fits the sofa exactly and has cording in the seams for a tailored appearance. Relaxed throws over the armchairs are quite a bit more casual—and perfect for an active family. Patterns for making a variety of slipcovers are available at most fabric stores.

Summer House

Slipcovering Hints

Enjoy combining mismatched furniture and don't confine yourself to pieces you already have. Search for gently used chairs or sofas with good lines and for pieces with simple easy-to-fit shapes. Fabric and crafts stores sell a variety of decorative trimmings, including buttons, braids, fringes, medallions, tassels, and rosettes.

Fluff up saggy cushions by wrapping them in batting before covering. Change the contour of a chair by adding layers of batting to the back and arms; batting will cling to the chair by itself, so it's not necessary to staple or sew it on.

Add soft cording, made of cotton welt encased in bias-cut fabric strips, between seams to define shapes, improve fit, and give a crisp and professional-looking edge. Ready-made cording can also be purchased in a variety of colors. The cording can either contrast with or match the fabric.

Lighthearted Living Hand-painted slipcovers in pale tones of pink, blue, and yellow provide cool comfort in this sun-drenched Florida living room created by artist/designer Carrie Raeburn. To create the repetitive designs on the cotton-duck fabrics, Carrie applied acrylic paints with sponges, brushes, and a variety of other implements. In most instances, she added the designs to the completed slipcovers, rather than painting the fabric beforehand. The instructions for painting fabric are on *page 86.*

Ocean Breezes Simple window treatments, such as valances used without curtains, are the order of the day. In this particular beach community, in fact, one covenant is that windows must remain uncovered during the day. This promotes a good exchange—marvelous views seen from the houses and an open, nonintimidating facade seen from the street. Like most houses in the area, this one requires minimum upkeep. Sweep-clean floors, area rugs, and washable fabrics keep the sand at bay.

Modern Classic

Soft, But Sophisticated This restful room has a monochromatic scheme with one color—green—in a range of values and intensities. A healthy dose of black adds visual weight, keeping the room from seeming too light in color. Neutrals add a little relief from the green. With such a minimal range of color, it's essential to incorporate textures, patterns, and interesting furniture shapes to keep the room from becoming dull. The success of this room comes from multiple fabrics and designer touches such as chunky trims and pockets on the curtains and slipcovers. Pillows, too, have their share of details, with moss fringes and artfully pieced fabric adding to the overall effect.

For a classic room with a contemporary twist, choose fabrics with geometric and patterned designs in colors with subtle contrast. Note that not all fabric called "natural-color" is the same—some tones might be slightly more yellow or green, so create a grouping with swatches of all fabrics and trims to see how they work together before purchasing. Also, look at the samples in different parts of the room at different times of the day to see how daylight and artificial light affect the colors.

Aside from the square topper on the round table, the other black touches are subtle—picture frames, a band on the carpet, a lamp shade, and a tray table used as a coffee table.

Parson's Chair
The slipcovers are made with Vogue pattern #1596, but the basic pattern is only a starting place. Here, a gusseted pocket accents the back, and stylish trim surrounds the seat. The instructions for making this slipcover is on *page 87*.

Fit and Trimmed Combinations of designer fabrics and lush trims make these pillows and chairs far more appealing than plainer varieties. Piece two or three fabrics together or center a printed motif in one panel of a pieced pillow, *right,* to create endless options to standard fabric-by-the-yard. A floor-length round tablecloth with a square topper, *below,* covers an inexpensive wooden table. The instructions for the tablecloth and topper are on *pages 87.*

Pillow Talk

Endless Options Fabric pillows can be a cost-effective way to achieve a coordinated look. While you might choose less costly fabrics to cover larger pieces of furniture, you can splurge on small pieces of expensive fabric to make designer pillows without emptying your wallet.

Overscale Furniture In some instances, large-scale furniture is too deep for comfortable seating. Luckily, large, comfortable pillows provide the best solution to the problem. Place pillows across the back of the seat to take up some of the extra space.

In a Snap For easy bedmaking, try a casually tossed grouping of pillows at the head of the bed. Place a pair of standard pillows in back, centered by a square European pillow on its corner. If a pillow lands a bit out of place, it doesn't matter—this is casual.

Sumptuous Look Try stacking pillows vertically in graduated sizes. For example, start with a pair of large pillows and top with a pair of smaller ones. Or, pile standard pillows atop king-size pillows and top with a pair in the 12×16-inch boudoir size. The instructions for making your own pillows are on *page 88.*

Shabby Chic

Playfully Shabby Behind the slipcovered chaise, *opposite,* a weathered French door leans against the plate glass window, and a draped curtain enhances the romantic effect of the vignette created. The pillows plumping up the back of the chaise are new, but they appear old because tea-dyed fabric and fabric turned to the wrong side were used in their construction. Rough-framed mementos hang from a ribbon, and an old column made into a lamp with a scrim shade attests to the wisdom of using found objects for decoration. The instructions for aging the fabrics, making the shade and lamp base are on *pages 88–90.*

Vintage Linens The key to achieving the right mix of white pillows is to vary the shades—from bright white to cream and taupe—and to make sure there is texture. The pillows *above* have dainty white linen over coarser oatmeal-color linen pillows. Search antique stores for old doilies or embroidered dresser scarves, and use them as decorative elements on solid pillows. Attach the two pieces with buttons or simply sew on some shiny pearl buttons for decoration.

Eastern Opulence

The Zen of Gilding Accessories graced with Asian motifs set the stage for the very luxurious living room, *opposite.* Opulent pillows, a velvet throw, and a stunning screen with silken panels have intricate golden designs adapted from a copyright-free book of Chinese motifs. Faux-finish walls, a pagoda-fretwork cornice, and gold-leafed candles further enhance the room.

The Midas Touch Gold metallic paint adds glamour to silk and velvet furnishings. To make the standing screen, *above,* the designer hand-painted free-form images on the silk panels with an artist's brush. For multiple images that are uniform in shape, such as those on the velvet pillow, use some of the many Eastern-motif stamps that are available. The instructions for painting these items are on *pages 90–91.*

Traditional Elegance

Dreamy Combination The juxtaposition of flowered fabrics and deep-pastel colors makes the room *opposite,* an inviting place. One fabulous fabric, used in abundance, ties the room together, and coordinating fabrics round out the mix. Large floral designs, such as the bouquets on the Parson's chair, should usually be centered, and all the repeats that are on one piece should be aligned. Tailored details on the chair and ottoman slipcovers, pillows, and draperies are an easy way to add a designer touch to the room. The instructions for all projects are on *pages 91–93.*

Flowing Drapery Hanging from a wooden rod with golden finials, the easy-to-sew draperies *below,* have a contrasting lining that ties in with fabrics used elsewhere in the room. The instructions for making these drapes are on *page 91.*

Definitive Details Designer touches on the slipcovers, made using a simple pattern, add immensely to the customized appearance of the room. Contrasting gussets, handsome fringes, woven braids, and closures made from corded tassels and covered buttons embellish basic slipcovers. The instructions for making decorative sewing details are on *page 92*.

Hand-Painted Credenza Gilded stenciling highlights the stunning credenza *opposite*, which picks up the leafy green and cream of the floral fabric. The instructions for painting the credenza are on *pages 92–93*.

Chair Affair

Monogram Magic Slipcover a wooden chair with a tailored topper that heralds the family name. Resembling a Swedish pinafore with dual layers of fabric, crocheted lace, piping at the seams, and a gracefully arched hem edged with ribbon, the slipcover, *right,* is an elegant improvement. To create your own version of the chair, choose a medium-weight taupe-and-cream gingham and ivory linen. Arch the hem only slightly, or the ribbon won't lie flat (small gathers in the ribbon will help). Machine-sew the monogram or have one made on the fabric before sewing the slipcover.

Art to the Rescue Reupholster an old chair with paintable canvas (from a fabric store) instead of carting an old chair to the trash. Let your artistic instincts take over by painting the canvas freehand or by tracing an image onto fabric using a slide projector. Adapt the instructions for painting fabric on *page 86* to create these one-of-a-kind slipcovers.

before

before

you were here

Fresh Update
Much more affordable than upholstering furniture, slipcovers offer many options. Darker fabric under a sheer fabric highlights the pattern in the top layer. To make the looped trim, pin 2½- to 3-inch loops of ribbon to bias tape. Cover the ends with another piece of bias tape and stitch through all layers. Use the ribbon trim at the bottom of the chair just as you would any other fringe.

Creative Curtains and Drapes

Pretty Patchwork A colorful patchwork shade—made from paper-backed silk usually used to bind books—shimmers on this pair of standard windows. Random six-inch squares cut from the silk create punches of color that are less predictable and far more interesting than a more orderly approach. Use fusible interfacing to iron the squares onto a standard roll shade with the edges touching. If any of the background shows between the squares, hide it with strips of ribbon attached to fusible tape. The instructions for making the patchwork shade are on *pages 93–94*.

Uptown Elegance
A beaded valance lends the crowning touch to windows framed by pull-back panels. Lined silk-blend panels—a surprise find at a chain home-improvement store— get a dramatic makeover with a few simple changes. The instructions for making the panels are on *page 94*.

Long and Toile Tab-top panels from a home improvement center get a French accent with buttons and panels made of three country prints. Using ready-mades keeps sewing to a minimum and requires less of costly designer fabrics. The instructions for making the tab-top panels are on *page 94.*

Silken Panels Department store draperies have never looked better than with a few additions to add more style. Gold-and-black buttons adorn each pleat, and silky fringe and a pencil-thin strip of checked fabric accent two edges of each panel. Two tie-backs on each side combine for a more opulent look. In the center, an easy-to-sew mock-Austrian shade made of shimmering dupioni silk finishes the treatment. The instructions for making the mock-Austrian shade are on *page 95.*

Garden Variety Combine and refashion discount-store coordinates to create a stylish window treatment. Three place mats top the drapery panels to form a pelmet, or shaped valance, stapled to a board. Combinations of stripes, florals, checks, and solids in the same color scheme create an infinite range of decorating possibilities that coordinate with other furnishings. The instructions for making the pelmet are on *page 95*.

simply
Kitchens

The kitchen is still the heart of the home. Whether yours has charming vintage character or even includes an up-to-date home office, you can add a personal touch by making these clever projects.

French Roosters

Free-Range Chickens Plump yellow hens add their cheerful presence to formerly plain windows over the sink *above.* Ready-made café curtains, newly stenciled with fabric paints, hang from a wooden pole—and a country-print scalloped valance is a sunny complement. Above the counter, two stenciled bulletin boards provide a neat way to display photos and the messages that accumulate in every kitchen. The instructions for stenciling the hens are on *page 96.*

French Roosters Guests won't stop crowing about how cleverly you've stenciled the kitchen chairs and walls with proud roosters flaunting their plumage, *opposite.* Chair seats are upholstered in a French-country fabric, with backs in natural muslin that serves as a perfect canvas for the painted design. The instructions for making the chair seats are on *page 96.*

A Kitchen with Color

Bright and Sunny Organize your recipes, bills, lists, and mail with a bulletin board that also has pockets. Coordinating furnishings include a reversible runner, a chair with a slipcovered back and a generous ruffled seat cushion, a perky lamp shade, and curtain panels that "tie back" with buttons to let in lots of natural light. The instructions for making all of these projects are on *pages 96–101.*

Fabric selection is important when making several items that will be used together. The fabrics should look good together and also be functional. Sturdy cotton or cotton blends are the best choices for most everyday furnishings. Prewashing the fabrics before sewing the items will prevent any shrinkage that could occur with the inevitable need to launder items used in the kitchen.

Home Headquarters

Pocket Board Little things like letters, bills, receipts, and notepads have a tendency to be strewn across a desk or clutter the kitchen unless there's a good place to store them. Put everything in its place with this handy, wall-hung storage board—twelve roomy pockets keep everything close-at-hand yet tidy. The instructions for making a pocket board are on *page 102.*

Executive Post Long hours spent at a desk or in front of a computer won't seem so hard with this tufted chair cushion and back-friendly lumbar pillow, *above.* Solids and stripes combine with smart polka dots to create a fresh look for the home office, *opposite.* A storage board for smaller items keeps clutter to a minimum. The instructions for making these projects are on *pages 101–103.*

Window Dressings

Mustard-Dyed Curtains Spice up plain fabrics with a staple that's probably in your fridge—yellow mustard. The squeeze bottle that aims the mustard onto the hot dog will also let you create a tracery of fine, mustard-yellow designs on linens for the kitchen. As anyone who has ever tried to get a mustard stain out of Junior's shirt will tell you, the color is very durable. The instructions for making the curtains *above,* are on *page 103.*

A New Calling Almost any attractive piece of fabric can become a window treatment if it's the right size. The light, airy curtain at *right,* was once a lace tablecloth. Choose fabric that is wider than your window and at least the length from the curtain rod to the floor. If the fabric or tablecloth is too long, fold over the top to create a valance. Hang the curtain from a rod with clip-on drapery rings. If you wish, gather the curtain toward the center and tie it with a ribbon.

Towel Shades Mix-and-
match linen towels are
always at home in the
kitchen, and never more so
than when dressing the
windows. The instructions
for making these multicolor
shades are on page *103*.

Harlequin Topper Opaque and sheer fabrics team up in this dramatic window treatment. The diamond-pattern valance is a bold accent for the kitchen window; a striped sheer, attached with ribbons laced through brass grommets, is its delicate complement. Two sheer panels hang to the floor, and the top layer of fabric is cinched at the waist with 1-inch-wide sheer ribbon.

Tying the Knot Traditional matchstick blinds have rarely looked so stylish as the ones *below,* secured with decorative fabric ties that match the kitchen color scheme. This treatment works best on shades that usually stay at the same level, although they can also be raised and lowered when necessary.

For each tie, cut one 7½-inch-wide fabric strip equal to twice the length of the window. With right sides facing, fold each strip in half lengthwise. Using a ½-inch seam allowance and leaving an opening on the long edge for turning, sew across each end of the strip and along the long edge. Turn the tie right side out and hand-sew the opening closed; press. Loop each tie over the blinds and tie the ends into a bow. Or, for a no-sew alternative, press each fabric strip under ½ inch on all edges, then press lengthwise with the wrong sides together, sandwiching fusible tape between the edges to adhere them. Ribbon can be used instead of fabric ties.

All Buttoned Up Transform cloth napkins into attractive (and easily washable) curtains, *below.* You'll usually need two to four napkins per panel, depending on the size of the window and the size of the napkins. Fold and stitch a rod pocket at the top of one napkin per panel. Overlap the bottom of that napkin with the top of another and sew five evenly spaced buttons through both layers. Continue adding napkins and buttons until the panels are the right length.

simply
Bedrooms

Whether it's warm, cozy, and filled with favorite things—or as simple and serene as a cloudless day—the bedroom is one area of the home that can be as personal as you like. Comfort, after all, should be comfortable for *you.*

Crisp in Green

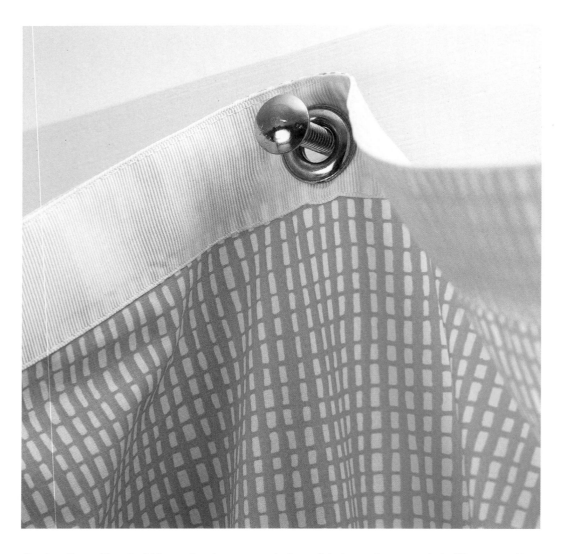

Springtime Fresh When sheets are made from fabric pretty enough to lift your spirits, use them in abundance! Sheet fabric is wide, it is always washable, and when compared to fabric-by-the-yard, it is relatively inexpensive. Green windowpane-check sheets drape both windows and walls in this bedroom that awakens to morning sun.

At the windows, sheers and shutters offer privacy, so the surrounding drapery remains undisturbed. Practical sheers are airy, nearly transparent fabrics usually made from cotton or synthetic fibers. Hang them from a simple rod to bring light into a dreary room, to block unfortunate views, and to minimize glare.

Metal grommets held up by carriage bolts anchored in the walls provide a novel way to hang the ribbon-bordered sheet-fabric panels, which are easily removed for laundering. On the bed, some sheets are used as bed linens, including a duvet cover, while others are cut and pieced to make pillows. Adapt the instructions on *page 104* to make the duvet cover.

Serene Slumber

Pillows Propping yourself up to read or talk on the telephone is a lot of fun when you can choose from all sorts of pillow shapes. The oversized pillow, a medium-size pieced pillow, and a small envelope pillow offer comfortable alternatives. The instructions for making the pillows are on *pages 106–107.*

Duvet Cover and Bed Skirt

Rejuvenate an old comforter by dressing it in a stylish new fabric cover, called a duvet. The reversible cover *right,* has a feminine toile on one side and more masculine checks on the other, in a perfect marriage of colors. No bed is completely dressed without a bed skirt draped over the boxspring. The gathered bed skirt *above,* is easy to make with the help of shirring tape. The instructions for making the duvet cover and bed skirt are on *pages 104–105.*

Haberdasher Style

All Shirted Up Striped or solid, smooth or textured, button-down or formal—that pile of worn and outgrown shirts provides the makings for unique pillows and bed linens. Even torn or stained shirts no longer suitable for wearing as garments contain a surprising amount of usable fabric to piece together for pillows and other projects in boys' rooms. Make shirt-patch pillows similar to those at *left,* with collars and cuffs for interest and front-button panels for closures. When it's time to do the laundry, simply unbutton the covers and throw them into the washing machine. Matching the pillows, a quilt and pillowcase borders are also made from shirt fabric. The instructions for making the shirt-front pillow is on *page 107.*

Lavender Dream

Flower Shower For a no-sew treatment behind the headboard, start with a shower curtain that matches your sheets. The shower curtain *left,* has an attached valance for added interest at the top but is the standard 72-inch-square shape. It hangs from drawer pulls attached to the wall and coordinates with pillow shams made from an extra curtain. The bed skirt, made from sheeting fabric, covers empty space beneath the bed, allowing it to be used for storage of out-of-season clothes. See *pages 108–109* for the wall hanging and bed skirt instructions.

Crowning Glory Charming in a guest room or romantic in the bedroom of a little princess, the half-moon canopy, *opposite,* lends a much-needed vertical accent to a small room dominated by a bed. Soften the wall behind the canopy with another panel draped from the ceiling or hang a favorite painting in the newly created niche. Although this room has numerous fabrics, its mood is still restful because the palette is limited to similar shades of one color. The instructions for making the canopy are on *page 108.*

Under Cover

Contemporary Cover-Up Tastes do change, and the headboard you used to love may now look out-of-date but could still be in good condition. Soften its appearance with a no-sew cover-up that drapes over the top. Cut a sheet 2 inches wider than the top of the headboard and long enough to hang over the front and back. (A twin sheet made the cover *above,* even easier because it could be turned on its side and simply folded in half.) Press under the raw edges and fuse in place with iron-on hemming tape. Sew ribbons to the sides and tie to hold the fabric in place.

Designer Discount Dressing an inviting bed is easy—and it need not break the bank. For the canopy *opposite*, buy inexpensive sheets for the panels but splurge on designer fabric for the narrow edgings and ties. Build a bed-size rectangular frame from 1×2-inch lumber. Staple the finished panels to it and suspend it from the ceiling with four hooks.

Cushy Comfort

Tailored for Comfort Lean back against a padded headboard made of thick foam. With a zip-off cover for easy cleaning, this soft substitute for a headboard also eliminates the need for piles of pillows. To keep the headboard in place, loop fabric over decorative drawer knobs anchored on the wall.

A Rose is a Rose Dress a bedroom chair in a romantic slipcover made of velvet with a prepleated silk skirt. Scatter tiny fabric roses, available from fabric stores, at intervals around the skirt. Make the matching cabbage-rose pillow by folding an 8-inch-wide strip of fabric lengthwise and then threading lightweight wire between the layers. Spiral the fabric, shaping it into a large rose, and sew it on top of a 12-inch round pillow covered in matching silk.

Mad for Monograms

Soft and Sweet Baby is not the only one who will love the cuddly comfort of this fleece "blankey"—his parents will also appreciate that it's personalized with Baby's name and birth date. Use the basic instructions on *page 109* to make larger fleece blankets or throws as gifts for newlyweds on your gift list as well.

Auntie's Hankie

Many vintage handkerchiefs already have an embroidered monogram, *right*. Other hankies, too, have colorful designs of flowers or scenes that are appropriate for decorating. Just iron the hankie and sew it to an existing pillow or attach it with buttons so it's removable for washing.

Cuddle-Up Comfort Two layers of cozy fleece ensure that family members will be warm as toast through the winter. To make the comforter, cut two pieces of fleece to the same size (one width by 2 yards is ideal). Pin the layers together with safety pins. Cut each side into matching 1-inch-wide strips and join the layers by knotting the strips in a consistent manner.

Fancy Blanket Borders Serviceable wool or acrylic blankets are almost necessities for cold or blustery nights, but that doesn't mean these staples of the linen closet can't be pretty as well. With add-on edgings of velvet, satin, brocade, or even faux fur, they gain that certain cachet that sets them apart from their more ordinary counterparts. An assortment of designer fabrics teams up with patchwork techniques, buttons, fringe, and metallic threads for even more "oomph" on the blankets, *opposite* and *below*. If these elaborately pieced borders are beyond your requirements, there are plenty of attractive trims in the notions department of any fabric store, including ribbons, rickrack, and many types of braid. Or, cut a narrow strip of fabric to match other items in the room and use a zigzag stitch to attach it to the blanket. Just be sure to consider the care instructions of the blanket (whether it's dry-cleanable or machine-washable) and choose compatible fabrics and trims. The instructions for adding these borders are on *pages 110–112.*

Sheers, Curtains & Scarves

High Drama A bed gains importance with contrasting fabric-lined curtains hung above the headboard, *opposite,* as though it's a window. Standard 84-inch-long curtains hang on a wooden rod supported at the ends and in the middle by wooden brackets. At each side of the headboard, matching finials, mounted to the wall studs, hold back the curtains with a ribbon loop. When seasons change, reverse the curtains for a new look and tie them back to create eye-catching contrast.

Case Study Take advantage of the decorative hems and simple construction of pillowcases to create charming window treatments. A cutwork pillowcase over one with a floral fabric and a ruffled edge looks like a pretty pinafore, *above.*

Cut one cutwork pillowcase, and also a ruffled pillowcase, along the sides and top. Align them so the ruffle hangs beneath the cutwork edge, trimming them at the top to fit the size of the window. Cut five 12-inch ribbon pairs for each panel; on the wrong side of the ruffled piece, sew the ribbons to the top with loose ends toward the ruffle. Place the right side of the cutwork piece on the wrong side of the ruffled piece; sew them at the top. Flip the cutwork piece toward the front. Hem the sides with double-folded ¼-inch hems. Tie the ribbons around the rod.

Ribbon Revival With a trip to a fabrics or crafts store yielding so many decorating possibilities in the form of ribbon and flat-weave braid, you'll never have to settle for plain white curtains again. Enhance ready-made panels *above,* with vertical lengths of ribbon, topstitching them along both edges and forming large loops of ribbon at the top. Cut the loops and tie the ends around a curtain rod to hang.

Faux Four-Poster Bring a touch of the islands to any bedroom with an exotic four-poster fashioned entirely from fabric, *left.* Lengths of lightweight fabric hanging from four circular finials form a restful retreat that will inspire you and yours to forget the rest of the world. The instructions for making the fabric four-poster are on *page 112.*

Sleek Retreat Serene in its simplicity, one dramatic swoop of gauzy fabric lends a sophisticated note by framing the bed, *opposite.* A chrome towel ring at each side attaches to the ceiling with only one screw, keeping the ceiling virtually unmarred. Mount the towel rings above the outer points of the headboard. (Measure the headboard first, then mark the width on the ceiling.) Hem the ends of a length of sheer gauzy fabric (eight or nine yards for a queen-size bed), and loop the fabric through the rings. The instructions for making the gauze canopy are on *page 108.*

Sweet Confirmation As sheer as the veil on a young girl's head, the canopy *right,* adds a lovely finish to a pristine white bedroom. To make the canopy, mount a scarf holder, available at curtain retailers, above the center of the headboard. Thread 6 yards of inexpensive sheer fabric through the holder and fan it out behind the bed, draping the fabric edges over the headboard.

simply Kids' Rooms

There's no better place to put sewing skills to work than in your precious darling's bedroom. An attractive room helps inspire a child—because creativity begins early.

Chenille Kid's Room

Sentimental Favorite Instead of keeping sentimental items hidden in boxes in the attic, look for innovative ways to showcase them. Vintage doll clothes, *right* and *opposite,* hang from a ribbon clothesline above the French doors, completely out of the way of little hands. Another idea: Use a well-secured peg rack to hang toys or photos above a changing table to keep baby occupied.

Tab Top Valance Cheery yellow chenille plus tabs and banding sewn from different fabrics add homespun charm to the tab-top valance, *right* and *opposite.* Because the patterns and colors aren't suited only for a baby, the fabrics offer plenty of decorating possibilities down the road when your child is older. The instructions for making the tab-top valances are on *page 113.*

Childhood Haven Bright pastel colors and textured surfaces go a long way toward creating a happy-looking room, *opposite,* that inspires creative play. The braided rug is soft enough for little knees, and the bed, piled high with pillows and quilts, is perfect for sleeping and afternoon naps. A comfy chair, slipcovered in a patchwork assortment of fabrics, ensures that grown-ups will have a place to read bedtime stories. Curtains at the window, topped with a clever valance, and shirred panels on the pair of doors provide privacy and light control.

Baby Sweet Dreams

Friendly Frogs When babies start to notice their surroundings, they become very conscious of smiles. This frisky crib companion, *left*, jumps for joy across the checkered pastel bumper pads surrounding baby's mattress. The instructions for making the bumper pads are on *pages 113–115*.

Tailored Crib Skirt Pastel dots and ball fringe lend a whimsical touch to the almost floor-length skirt hanging beneath the crib, *left* and *opposite*. Inverted pleats and a solid band at the bottom are tailored touches that add to the overall neat appearance of your child's room. The instructions are on *pages 115–116*.

Pastel Beginnings When the family comes home from the hospital, this sweetly old-fashioned room ensemble is set up and ready to receive the new baby. Everything goes together: The bumper pads and crib skirt, the window valance, and the lamp shade cover are made from fabrics that blend. A warm blanket, also shown on *page 54,* even has baby's name embroidered on the side.

Pocket Helper Two roomy pockets made from chenille hold a multitude of items in the nursery. Hang the pockets on the wall above the changing table and fill them with diapers. Or fasten the hook-and-loop straps over the arm of a rocking chair to keep bedtime stories close and ready. Any way you choose to use it, this versatile organizer will add welcome order to your child's room. The instructions for making the pocket helper are on *page 117*.

Shed Some Light

Dress up the lamp in your child's room by painting it to match the furniture and adding a crisp fabric shade cover to the existing shade. Ball fringe and an embroidered edging add just the right decorative touches to the simple shape. The instructions for making the lamp are on *page 118*.

Top of the Morning

Sunshine streams through the nursery windows, casting a warm light inside. A cheery valance gathered on a rod coordinates with the tailored crib skirt, adorned with the same ball fringe. The instructions for the valance are on *page 116*.

Counting the Lamps Little lambs cavort among the stars in this room filled with appliquéd projects any new mother would appreciate. Hone your skills with machine-piecing and machine-appliqué to create a decorative set for baby that includes pieced bumper pads, a pillow, a wall quilt, and a valance. The instructions for these projects are on *pages 118–123*.

One Lamb, Two Lamb Two fluffy lambs float through a quilted sky on the delightful wall quilt, *above,* that's designed to encourage peaceful dreams and restful sleep. Babies love watching their little-lamb friends on this checkerboard-bordered wall hanging. The instructions for making the quilt are on *page 118.*

Lamb Bumper Pads Babies seem to have sweeter dreams when they sleep surrounded by favorite stuffed animals, at home with the Little Lamb bedding, *right.* The pillow features the checkered border and star appliqués found on the bumper pads, and a leaping lamb guides your baby to the gentle land of Nod. The instructions for the bumper pads, pillow, and matching valance are on *pages 120–123.*

Roll With It

Warmth at the Window Add a practical touch with a roller shade made from thick fleece that acts like a winter coat to keep Jack Frost outside where he belongs. Decorative edge-stitching provides casual contrast to the cheerful red fleece. Raise and lower the shade by rolling it up manually, using the buttons on the adjustable twill straps to hold it in place. Cut a piece of fleece to the exact width needed, and also to the exact length, plus about six inches. Adapt the instructions for making fabric-tied kitchen shades on *page 38,* but instead of using fabric strips as ties, hang twill straps at the front and back of the shade, sewing them at the top. Tack buttons to the front strap, and sew a buttonhole at the lower end of the back strap. Wrap and staple the bottom of the shade around a strip of ¼-inch-thick lattice cut to size. Cut a 1×2-inch board to the inside width of the window; staple the finished shade to the top side, and screw it into the window frame from the bottom.

Under the Big Top

Big Time at the Big Top
Bring laughter and fun to a child's room by turning a simple wardrobe into a storage unit fit for a budding circus performer. Cut a tent-shape piece of plywood, cover it with batting and then bright fabric, and attach it like a cornice to the front of the cabinet. Staple fabric on the back of the cabinet, and hang a narrow matching panel behind the cornice at each side.

simply
Bathrooms

Today's bathroom is often a soothing oasis of tranquility, where a warm bath, fragrant oils, and softer amenities go a long way toward creating a relaxed frame of mind.

Toile Expressions

Buttoned Border
Black-and-white checks and button-pinched tabs are smartly finished details at the top of the shower curtain, *left*. The instructions for making the border are on *page 125*.

Pretty, but Practical
Create an unmistakably elegant bathroom display by adding unique trims to solid-color towels, combining antique linens with new finds, and then hanging them all on a handsome rack, *right*.

Black 'n White Roman Shade
A Roman shade covered with classic toile fabric would be pretty enough alone, but here it soars to another decorative level with a trim of crystal prisms that catch the light, *lower right*. The instructions for making the shade are on *page 126*.

Opposites Attract A newly redecorated bath packs a powerful punch—created with well-placed color, pattern, and texture. Dramatic black-and-white is in stark contrast with the pastel-pink antique plates used as accessories.

Comfortable Chenille

Cozy Comfort
Chenille accents transform an all-white bathroom to a vibrant space that fairly sings with excitement, as towels, a trimmed wastebasket, and even an throw rug add to the effect. The muted tones of fuzzy chenille depend on the colors of the original cotton fabrics—layering the fabrics in a different order results in some very surprising differences. Make the chevron-pattern area rug with six-inch squares of fabric and then sew strips of chenille to bathroom accessories. The instructions for making the chenille projects are on *pages 124–125.*

Clever Cover-Up Disguise damaged walls and unsightly plumbing pipes with yards and yards of billowing fabric. Staple fabric to wooden strips fastened to the top and bottom of the walls, and dress the sink in a floor-length skirt that also hides necessities. Adapt the instructions for making the sink skirt on *page 126.*

Queenly Splendor Drape an everyday tub with an elegant tent of lined fabric, hanging on brackets that project from the wall. This may be a time to opt for inexpensive fabric, but buy enough to create a luxurious effect.

Old Softie

A Place of Your Own
Slipcovered in soft and absorbent terrycloth, this dressing-room chair is so comfortable that it might become your favorite spot to relax. It's easy to care for too—whenever it needs to be washed, just throw it in with the towels.

From Bedspread to Bath
A lightweight, twin-size coverlet becomes a sleek, tailored shower curtain, *below,* that coordinates with the bed in the adjoining room. To keep the fabric dry, just hang a clear plastic liner from the same clips; the reversible plaid is just as pleasing seen from inside the tub.

Avant-Garde Alternative When the shower curtains found in stores begin to seem all too predictable, try creating one to suit your own tastes. Look for photo-transfer paper at crafts stores or computer stores. Follow the manufacturer's instructions to create transfers from any images. Iron the transfers onto a plain shower curtain for a unique reflection of your interests. The one *above* features pictures of chairs from an office furniture catalog.

New Attitude

Skirt the Issue A no-fuss gathered sink skirt, *left,* is a graceful alternative to less-than-attractive undersink plumbing. It's also an efficient way to extend storage space. Use hook-and-loop fastening tape to attach the skirt to the sink. A finished band at the top can be mounted either on the front edge of the sink or under the lip, determined by which side of the band the tape is sewn. The instructions for making the sink skirt are on *page 126.*

Dramatic Impact Two panels frame the bathtub to create a semi-enclosed area that feels more intimate and less exposed than if it were open to the rest of the room. The multifabric panels hang from ties on ceiling-mounted hooks to function much like an immobile shower curtain. Coordinating accessories complement the panels. To make similar panels, adapt the instructions for making the Button-Back Curtains on *page 100.* The rug has three layers: Sew the fabric to a piece of latex nonslip rug liner with a layer of polyester quilt batting between them and cording around the edges. Quilt through all the layers for a rug that feels heavenly underfoot.

Simply
Instructions

Making soft and comfy home furnishings is even more fun now. With clear instructions, helpful diagrams, and your own skills and imagination, you can create new and exciting ideas for every room. Refer to *page 126* for the resource guide.

Lighthearted Living Painted Sham
Shown on pages 8–9

Supplies
- 100-percent-cotton or polyester/cotton pillow sham, prewashed
- Permanent fabric paint
- Colorless extender
- Jars for mixing paint, one per color
- Plastic bags for lining sham
- ¾"-wide masking tape
- Paintbrushes for acrylics: various round-tip and stiff-bristle brushes
- 1"-wide sponge brush
- Household sponges, cut into rounds, triangles, or other shapes for detailing
- Shallow white plates for paint palettes
- Paper towels for blotting

Color Suggestions
Orange-yellow and lemon yellow (for flower centers and stripes)

Clear pink, fuchsia, lavender, and peach (for flowers and rose details)

Blue-green, medium green, and light medium green (for swirl details, triangles, and leaves)

Turquoise blue (for checked border)

Start to Finish
Prepare to Paint: Use ready-mixed fabric paint or mix colors to obtain the desired shades. Thin each color with colorless extender and a small amount of water. It is highly recommended that you practice on a piece of fabric before starting the project.

To prevent paint from seeping onto the back, line the pillow sham with plastic bags, making sure the plastic extends into the corners. Measure and mark the top triangle with masking tape; the center of the point is slightly more than a third, but less than halfway, from the top. Measure and mark the stripes with masking tape. Also tape around the stitching line.

Paint the Fabric: Using a straight-edge sponge and a dabbing technique, paint the stripes and the flower centers in the triangle section, blotting any excess paint. Remove the masking tape between the stripes (see photo 1, *top right*), but leave it in place elsewhere.

Using various round-tip brushes and starting with the lightest hue, paint freehand flowers in a sweeping motion on the striped section. Complete all strokes of one color before beginning with another color.

Using a sponge and a stiff-bristle brush, paint the flower centers in lemon yellow and orange-yellow. For flowers in the triangle

(see photo 2, *right*), use a fairly stiff fan-shape brush, building the layers in sweeping strokes and going from light to dark hues. Holding a medium-size round brush upright and twirling the shaft between the fingers, paint an irregular swirled effect on each flower.

Sponge rosy circles and brush blue-green swirls on the striped section. Using a triangle-shape sponge as a stamp, paint leaves on the triangle section (see photo 3, *right*).

For the checked border, use a 1-inch-wide foam brush to lightly apply turquoise blue, leaving some white showing through (see photo 4, *right*); let it dry overnight. Remove the masking tape. Press the sham on the wrong side with a dry iron to set the color.

Parson's Chair
Shown on pages 10–13

Supplies
- Decorator fabrics
- Fabric for lining
- Decorator trim with woven band and wooden beads
- Vogue Pattern #1596
- Kraft paper
- Wood button

Start to Finish

Make the slipcover for the basic Parson's Chair following the instructions for Vogue pattern #1596. To make the 8-inch-square gusset pocket, first cut a rectangular pattern from kraft paper, allowing 2 inches for a gusset in the center and ½-inch seams on all sides. Cut one rectangle from coordinating fabric and one from lining fabric; sew them together with right sides facing, leaving an opening for turning. Turn the rectangle right sides out, and press the edges and the gusset.

Pin the pocket to the back of the slipcover and topstitch the sides and bottom, leaving an opening at the top. Measure the width of the finished pocket; and then cut a kraft-paper pattern for the flap, allowing for ½-inch seams all around. Cut one flap from the coordinating fabric and one from the lining fabric; sew the two pieces with right sides together, leaving a small opening for turning. Turn the flap and press.

Make a buttonhole through both layers. Pin the flap (with right sides facing and the buttonhole at the top) above the pocket and sew along the bottom edge. Fold the top toward the pocket; press. Sew a button to the pocket and button the flap.

The designer trim at the top of the skirt is a woven band with dangling wooden pieces. Other trims would work equally well.

Fit and Trimmed Skirted Table
Shown on pages 10–13

Supplies
- Decorator fabrics
- Pencil
- String

Start to Finish

Round Skirt: Measure the distance from the center of the table to the floor, plus enough for a hem (about 2 inches). Sew enough fabric (usually two widths) together lengthwise to form a piece of fabric wide enough for the round skirt.

Fold the fabric into quarters and pin one end of a string to the point that will be the center. Tie a pencil at the other end of the string with a loose knot; adjust the distance and tighten the knot at the point where the string equals the initial measurement.

Keeping the tension of the string and pencil steady, draw an arc around the fabric. Cut through the fabric, one layer at a time, along the penciled line; this will form a circular piece of fabric. Turn and press the hem ¼ inch toward the wrong side; then turn and press again to make a hem. Sew the hem; cover the line of stitching with decorative trim, if desired.

Square Topper: Measure the diameter of the table. Add from 16 to 24 inches (enough for the topper to hang 8 to 12 inches at each side) to obtain the final measurement. Using this measurement, cut a square from coordinating fabric. For a lined topper, cut another square from lining fabric. With right sides together, sew around the edges, leaving an opening for turning. Turn and press.

To finish the edges on an unlined topper, turn and press ½ inch toward the wrong side of each edge, then turn and press again; sew along each edge.

Soft, but Sophisticated Sheers

Shown on pages 10–11

Supplies
- Decorator fabric, sheer
- Decorator fabric, stripe for accent

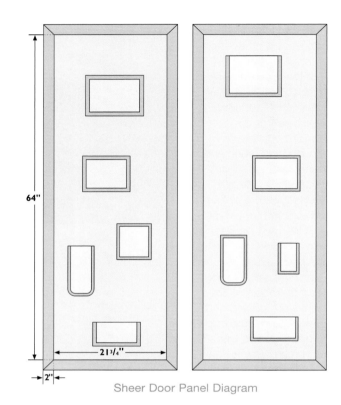

64"

21³/₄"

2"

Sheer Door Panel Diagram

Playfully Shabby Lamp

Shown on page 14–15

Supplies
- Wooden column or other object
- Metal lamp socket and harp kit
- Cap and base
- Threaded rod; washers; brass hex nut to fit rod
- Spacers and finial
- Lamp shade
- Sheer fabric or scrim
- Brass ring (slightly smaller than top of lampshade)
- Lace or trim
- Crystal prisms
- Drill and drill bits
- Needle-nose pliers
- Hacksaw
- Wire
- Masking tape

Start to Finish

To make the pocketed door panels, cut lengths of sheer fabric to cover the glass panes of a single or double door, allowing enough extra fabric to turn under for casings at the top and bottom and hems along each side. Cut a variety of pockets from the same fabric (see the Sheer Door Panel Diagram *above*).

Make Bias Strips: Cut 4½- and 1½-inch bias strips from the accent fabric. With wrong sides together, fold under and press ¼ inch along each edge; fold and press another crease down the center. Trim the panels and pockets with the bias strips. Sew the pockets to the panels. Make a casing at the top and bottom for each panel.

Fit and Trimmed
Shown on pages 11–13

Supplies
- Decorator fabrics
- Pillow forms
- Kraft paper
- Zipper
- Buttons, cording, trims, or tassels

Start to Finish

For each pillow, purchase a pillow form; measure the dimensions and add a 1-inch seam allowance to all sides. Cut a kraft-paper pattern to these measurements. To make a pieced top, fold the pattern in thirds, as for the palm tree, or in halves or quarters, depending on the design. Cut the pattern into sections; cut out sections from fabric, allowing extra fabric for seams. Measure the outside dimension and cut a back to fit.

Sew the top and back together, right sides facing. Insert a zipper or hook-and-loop fastening tape along one of the sides to close. Finish with buttons, cording, trims, or tassels.

Start to Finish

Purchase the metal lamp socket kit, a standard threaded rod, washers, a plug, and the component that holds the harp for the shade at a hardware store. Specialized parts, such as spacers and finials, are available at lamp shops.

Lamp Base: The column used to make the lamp shown on *page 14* was already hollow. If necessary, drill a hole through the column or other object from top to bottom. (A drill press works best for an accurate line-up; tough or fragile surfaces sometimes require specialized drill bits made for masonry or diamond-coated drill bits made for porcelain to avoid breakage.)

Choose a cap and a base that complement the shape of the lamp and will cover the drilled holes. Many caps and bases are commercially available, but anything that fits can be used to add individuality. Make sure the lamp base has room at the bottom for the metal components by drilling a 1-inch-wide and ½-inch-deep recessed area in the underside of the base, if necessary. Stack the components, including the socket and harp components, and measure the height from top to bottom, adding only enough for the rod to attach the metal components and subtracting enough for the bottom of the rod to recess ¼ inch from the bottom of the base. Using a hacksaw, cut a standard threaded rod to this measurement.

Decide where the cord should exit the lamp base. If the lamp has feet, leave the cord loose; otherwise, drill an exit hole in the back of the base.

Insert the rod through the drilled column or other object, the cap, and the base. Secure the cap and base with a washer. Thread the electrical cord through the rod and attach the metal

cap socket and harp holder to it; tighten securely. Add a plug to the end of the cord. Attach the harp. Insert a lightbulb into the socket and test it. Top the lamp with the shade and secure with the finial.

Lamp Shade Cover:
Measure the length of the lamp shade from the top to the bottom of the shade; allow enough extra length to sew a channel at the top for the ring, and for the cover to hang below the shade.

Cut each width of sheer fabric or scrim (a loosely woven fabric available in the drapery department of large fabric stores) to this length. Sew the pieces end to end to create one long loop with about three times the distance around the bottom of the lamp shade. Sew a ⅝-inch-wide channel along one cut edge and sew lace or other trim to the right side along the other cut edge.

Note: Brass rings are sold

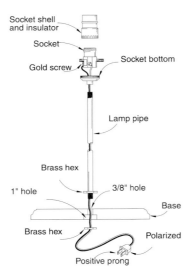

at fabric stores. Cut through the brass ring using a hacksaw; cover rough ends with masking tape. Thread the ring through the channel at the top edge of the sheer fabric or scrim (see *photo 1, below*). Place the fabric-covered ring on the top of the lamp shade and arrange the folds evenly.

For crinkled scrim, place a plastic bag over the original shade to protect it, then hang the scrim shade cover over the plastic cover. Lightly mist the shade cover with an even coat of water (see

photo 2), and let it dry before removing the plastic from the shade. The scrim fabric crinkles as it dries.

To recreate the effect of the dangling prisms on the lamp, drill tiny holes through the top of the lamp base. Insert a piece of wire in each hole; make a small loop at the top and the bottom of the wire with needle-nose pliers. Hang a prism from each bottom loop.

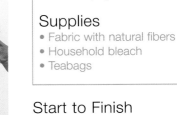

Playfully Shabby Fabric
Shown on page 14

Supplies
- Fabric with natural fibers
- Household bleach
- Teabags

Start to Finish
At least three methods—bleaching, tea-dying, and using the reverse side—can be used to adapt too-bright fabric to the soft colors for a shabby-chic style.

The pieced pillow on *page 14* has narrow strips from the right side of the fabric, side panels from the reverse side of the same fabric, and tea-dyed fabric in the center.

Buy fabrics with a large percentage of natural fibers, such as cotton, for best results, and experiment with a swatch before working on the fabric itself. Always stay-stitch the edges. Prewash the fabrics if they will be used in a sewing project that is likely to be washed. This is particularly important if they will be combined with other washable fabrics that may shrink at different rates.

Bleaching: (See photo 1.) The same bleach that whitens whites will work on bright colors to tone them down to the desired shade. Remember that all colors won't react to the bleach in the same way, which is why a swatch test is important. Mix the bleach in water according to the manufacturer's instructions and soak the fabric until the colors fade. Watch carefully, as colors may fade fast and will be even paler when the fabric dries. Rinse out the bleach thoroughly, dry, and iron the fabric.

Tea-dyeing: (See photo 2.) Soaking fabrics in tea (or sometimes coffee, for a different tone) is the time-honored way to create the slight sepia cast that older fabrics often have. Fill a one-gallon container half full of very hot tap water. Add 16 tea bags (or the equivalent) and steep 20 minutes. Soak the fabric in the warm tea, stirring and checking the color of the fabric every 5 minutes (most fabrics take from 10

to 35 minutes to absorb enough color). Either leave the fabric as is or rinse it to remove some of the color before placing it in the dryer with an old damp towel to absorb any residue. Press the fabric to set the color.

Using the Reverse Side: (See photo 3.) Many screen-printed fabrics have highly saturated colored designs on one side and a paler version on the other. The undersides of these fabrics are frequently just right for use in shabby-chic projects.

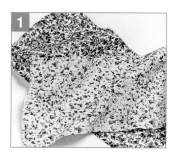

The Midas Touch
Shown on pages 16–17

Supplies
- Decorator fabrics such as silk and panne velvet
- Artist's acrylic paint: Pure Gold and Antique Gold Metallic
- Artist's paintbrushes: ¼" and ½" flats
- Assorted rubber stamps: Hot Potatoes—Fan #0314; Plaid Enterprises—Koi Fish #56321; American Traditional Stencils—Greek Key; Border Foam Stamp #74004
- American Traditional Stencils—Love & Happiness; Chinese Stencils #BL715
- Small sea sponge
- Tracing paper
- Transfer paper
- Heavy cardboard
- Foam sheet for padding
- Muslin
- T-pins

Start to Finish
Create the pillows, the throw, and the screen with three simple techniques: hand-painting from a pattern, stamping, and stenciling. Combine any or all of the techniques on individual projects, depending on the preferred effect. Paint yardages of fabric and let dry before constructing the item.

Because sizing creates a barrier between the fabric and the paint and may prevent a good bond, prewash the fabrics, if possible. (Do not prewash dry-cleanable fabrics such as silk and velvet.) If applying paint to prewashed purchased accessories, stretch the fabric flat and place heavy cardboard between the layers to keep wet paint from bleeding through the fabric.

Cover the work table with foam padding and then muslin; stretch the muslin toward the back, and secure it with tape. Stretch the fabric flat and secure it to the surface with T-pins.

Stamping and Stenciling: *Note: Practice on a scrap of fabric to determine the amount of paint needed on the stamp or stencil brush to create the desired effect.*

When stamping, apply the paint to the stamp with a small roller (see photo 1, *opposite*). For designs of even color, reapply paint with the roller before each impression. Fill in any missed areas by applying paint with a brush. Don't try to restamp—it's almost impossible to realign the design. Let the paint dry thoroughly, then heat-set the painted fabric.

Stencil the designs onto the stretched fabric, using Pure Gold and Antique Gold metallic paints and a good stencil brush or sponge (see photo 2). Let the paint dry thoroughly. Then heat-set the painted fabric.

Hand-Painting: Use artist's paintbrushes to hand-paint designs such as the one shown in photo 3. Trace a favorite image onto tracing paper and enlarge it by means of a copy machine or a grid to fit the project. Using transfer paper, transfer the design onto the stretched fabric. Carefully fill in the design, using Pure Gold and Antique Gold metallic acrylic paints and high-quality ¼-inch- and ½-inch-wide flat artist's paintbrushes. Let the paint dry thoroughly.

For silks and fabrics with no nap, heat-set the design by repeatedly pressing the reverse side with a dry iron set on medium heat. For velvets and other napped fabrics, heat-set the design by placing the fabric in a commercial dryer set on the highest setting for 30 to 45 minutes.

Dreamy Combination Pillow
Shown on page 19

Supplies
- Various decorator fabrics
- Pillow form
- Kraft paper
- Ruler and pencil
- Braid, fringe, or trim
- Tassel and button

Start to Finish
Measure the pillow form; cut a kraft-paper pattern to these measurements. Use a ruler and pencil to divide the pillow top into sections. Cut the sections apart and pin onto the fabrics. Cut out the pieces, allowing ½ inch on all sides from seam. Sew the pillow top together. Measure the completed pillow top and cut a back piece to match. Add braid or sew trim around the outer edge of the pillow top, if desired. Sew the two pieces together, leaving an opening for turning. Insert the pillow form and slip-stitch the opening closed. Sew on a tassel and button, if desired.

Flowing Drapery
Shown on pages 18–19

Supplies
- Decorator fabric (face)
- Decorator fabric (lining)
- Trim or fringe

Start to Finish
Note: This is a quick-sew drapery method: Each floor-length panel, consisting of the face fabric and a lining fabric, is sewn like a pillowcase, then turned right sides out and stitched closed at the top. The valance is sewn in the same manner, and then the two pieces are joined together.

Measure the distance from the top of the rod to the floor to obtain the length. The width should be 2½ times the width of the window (measure outside the window casing). For each panel, cut the face fabric and the lining fabric to the same length and width, piecing the lengths of fabric if necessary to obtain enough width. For each valance, cut two 16½-inch long pieces of coordinating fabric the same width as the panels.

With right sides together, pin and sew all four sides of the panel, leaving an opening for turning at the top. Clip the corners and turn. Slip-stitch the opening closed and press. Repeat to make the valance.

Sew fringe to the face fabric along one side and the bottom of the panel, mitering the corners (see Drapery Diagram *below*). Sew fringe to the face fabric along the two sides and bottom of the valance.

Drapery Diagram

Place the panel faceup and the valance facedown so the two sections overlap by 4 inches. Pin the edge of the valance to the panel (see the dashed line on the Drapery Diagram). Turn the drapery over and pin the panel edge to the valance to form the rod pocket. Before sewing the pocket down, insert the rod to check for size. The pocket should have at least ½ inch to ⅜ inch of ease for gathering or possible shrinkage. Adjust the overlap and sew the layers together.

Dreamy Combination Sewing Details

Shown on pages 18–20

Supplies
- Decorator fabrics
- Vogue Pattern #1904
- Various trims, braids, and tasseled cords
- Buttons
- Fabric glue

Start to Finish

Make the ottoman and chair slipcovers using Vogue pattern #1904, but also make a few simple changes: Choose an accent fabric to set off the inverted pleats of the chair slipcover and add trim or braid to cover the seams and a matching tassel version to finish the hem.

To close the pleats, as shown on the chair and ottoman on *pages 18–19*, use one of the following techniques: To make the half-cord closure, sew a button on the left side of the pleat. Cut the tasseled cord in half and dip the cut

end into fabric glue to eliminate fraying. After it has dried, fashion the cord into a Decorative Frog (see photo *below*), and sew it in place.

To make the whole-cord closure at *left*, sew a button on each side of the pleat, then loop the cord around the buttons, tying it first in a knot, and then in a bow.

To add interest to the ottoman, use a combination of formal and informal fabrics in colors that coordinate. Sew bulky looped fringe into the seam to frame the top, and add an 8-inch-long bullion fringe to finish the bottom.

Decorative Frog

Hand-Painted Credenza

Shown on pages 19–21

Supplies
- Wooden chest
- Medium- and fine-grit sandpaper
- Tack cloth
- Delta Ceramcoat Acrylic Paint: Lichen Grey 2118, Dark Forest Green 2096, Dark Chocolate 2021, Rain Forest Green 2462, Territorial Beige 2426, Santa Fe Rose 2496
- Paintbrushes: Large, flat brush (for base-coating) and small stencil brush
- Delta Ceramcoat 2-part Fine Crackle Finish, Step 1 and Step 2
- Antiquing medium (or clear glaze and black acrylic paint)
- Royal Design Studio Stencils: Parisian Swag Panel #810 and Toulouse #812
- 4"-wide paint roller
- Clear glaze
- Sea sponge
- Provo Craft Daisy Chain Stencil #41-8616
- Rub 'n Buff Gold Leaf
- Satin-finish acrylic varnish

Start to Finish

Note: Check local furniture stores for inexpensive imported furniture. Even if a piece is already finished, its cost may be comparable to that of an unfinished or old/antique piece.

If using a prefinished piece, sand it with medium- and then fine-grit sandpaper prior to painting to create enough "tooth" for the paint to adhere. Remove all sanding dust with the tack cloth.

Top: Base-coat the top of the wooden chest with two coats of Lichen Grey, allowing ample drying time between coats. Lightly sand and wipe away the sanding dust. Crackle-finish the top by applying the first coat of the 2-part crackle medium; let it dry according to the manufacturer's instructions. Apply Step 2 of the medium and allow it to dry overnight. *Note: A thin application of the crackle produces fine cracks; a thick application produces larger cracks. Brush the medium in both directions to encourage the eggshell-type cracks. Allow the full drying time. Rubbing the antiquing medium on any sooner moistens and moves the crackle medium.*

Antiquing: Age the top with antiquing medium (or use a small amount of clear glaze mixed into black paint; see photo 1).

Drawers and Doors: Remove the doors, drawers, and all hardware before painting the chest.

Base-coat only the outer surface of the drawers and the center panels of the doors with Lichen Grey. (Do not paint the edges or inside surfaces because the drawers and doors may stick with the added paint, or, in the case of unfinished furniture, may swell.) Lightly sand and wipe away the sanding dust.

Note: Adjust the stencils to fit the furniture. Some parts of the stencil were repeated on either side to add width. Align the drawers in order with the fronts facing up and plan the design accordingly. Use painter's tape to tape the Toulouse stencil to one drawer at a time; using the roller and Territorial Beige, stencil the design. Repeat for the Parisian Swag Panel on the doors. Let the paint dry thoroughly. Finish the drawers and doors with the crackle finish, following the instructions for the top.

Finishing Touches: Paint the routed edges or borders between the drawers, doors, top, and bottom with Santa Fe Rose. Randomly brush or sponge on Dark Forest Green.

Glaze the entire piece. Mix Dark Chocolate with clear glaze 1:1 and brush it onto the surface, working in one area at a time (see photo 2). Dampen a sea sponge and use to slightly remove some of the wet glaze to let the base colors show through. Pat away any "puddled" glaze with a paper towel and let the area

dry. With a cloth or sponge, randomly add Dark Forest Green, then Rain Forest Green over the top of the glaze (see photo 3).

Use painter's tape to attach the Daisy Chain stencil along the upper edge of the credenza and apply Rub 'n Buff according to the package instructions. Apply more Rub 'n Buff to accent all raised areas.

Finish with two or more coats of satin-finish varnish, allowing ample drying between coats. Reassemble the chest.

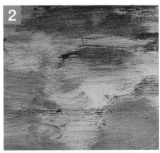

Pretty Patchwork Shade

Shown on page 24

Supplies
- Fabric roller shade, white
- Two-sided fusible interfacing
- Paper-backed silk (for binding books)
- Quilters grid
- Rotary cutter

Start to Finish

Note: Purchase a white fabric roller shade to fit the window (or purchase an iron-on shade kit at a fabric store). If using a regular white roller shade, also purchase enough two-sided fusible interfacing to equal the area of the shade. Paper-backed silk made for binding books is available at art stores.

Measure the length and width of the shade and divide each measurement by 6. Then multiply the resulting numbers to determine how many 6-inch-square pieces to cut. Using a quilter's grid and a rotary cutter for straight edges, cut squares of paper-backed silk in various colors and patterns. Iron the squares onto the shade so the edges of the squares touch and no white shows through (follow the manufacturer's instructions for ironing). Install the shade inside the window frame. *Note: Additional fabric may be needed for extra-wide windows.*

Uptown Elegance
Shown on page 25

Supplies
- Three 40×84" drapery panels
- 2½ yards of bead trim
- 1 yard of matching ribbon
- Six crystal knobs fitted with double-ended threads

Start to Finish
Cut one panel in half vertically to make two 40×42-inch-wide pieces for the valance. With wrong sides together, fold each piece in half to make a 20×42-inch-wide piece; press, and then sew the raw edges together. Sew the bead trim onto the folded edge of the valance.

Place one of the full-length panels right side up. Align the untrimmed edge of the valance with the top of the panel (see the Panel Assembly Diagram *below*); pin, and then sew together. Repeat for the other side. Fold each valance toward the front of the drapery panel and topstitch.

Cut the ribbon into 6-inch lengths. Sew the ribbon to make loops at the top edge of the drapery/valance, placing one in the center of each panel and one at each edge. Attach the crystal knobs to the wall above the window. Hang a ribbon loop from each knob.

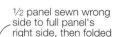

½ panel sewn wrong side to full panel's right side, then folded

Panel Assembly Diagram

Long and Toile Panels
Shown on page 26

Supplies
- Two 16×48" pieces of blue toile fabric
- Six 2"-wide strips of red fabric
- Six 5"-wide strips of yellow-and-red toile fabric
- Two 40×84" tab-top panels
- Ten buttons covered in red fabric

Start to Finish
Cut the blue toile fabric to the specified dimensions.

Cut the red strips on the bias and sew them together at the ends to make one long strip (see Bias Strips Diagram, *page 128*). Fold strip in half with wrong sides together and press. With cut-edge to the outside, pin the strip to all four sides of the blue toile panel. Miter the corners of the red strip as you pin, then sew. Press the red strip to the outside of the panel.

Cut the red-and-yellow toile strips on the bias and sew them together at the ends to make one long strip. Pin this strip to the folded edge of the red strip, with the right sides facing, mitering the corners, and stitch.

Baste a trimmed toile panel to the center of each curtain panel and topstitch in place (see Tab-Top Curtain Fabric Placement Diagram, *below*).

Replace the original buttons with the fabric-covered buttons.

Tab-Top Curtain Fabric Placement Diagram

Silken Panels and Mock-Austrian Shade

Shown on page 26

Supplies

- Pair of pinch-pleated draperies that fit the window
- Shank buttons; one for each pleat
- ½ yard small-check 54"-wide fabric
- 2½ yards 54"-wide large plaid fabric (for shade)
- Fringe for drapes
- Fabric tape
- Wooden rod with rings; drapery hooks
- Two tension rods to fit inside the window

Note: Additional fabric may be needed.

Start to Finish

Trimmed Draperies: Cut 2¼-inch-wide strips from the small-check fabric and sew the ends together to make two longer strips, each long enough to trim the side and the bottom of one panel. Fold the strip into thirds lengthwise and press. Sew the fringe along the center and bottom edges. Sew the fabric tape over the fringe to cover the woven edge of the fringe, mitering the corners and folding under the ends.

Sew a button at the base of each pleat. Install the wooden rod. Insert a drapery hook into each pleat to hang.

Mock Austrian Shade: Sew a narrow hem along each raw edge of the fabric for the shade. Make a 2-inch-wide rod pocket along each of the selvage edges to hold the two tension rods (see Mock Austrian Shade Diagram *below*). Insert one rod into each casing. Install the shade with one tension rod inside the casing at the top of the window and one rod about halfway down. Gather the fabric along the top rod and puff the fabric to drape over the front of the lower rod.

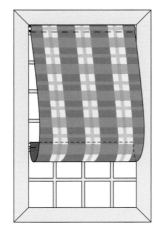

Mock Austrian Shade

Garden Variety Pelmet

Shown on page 27

Supplies

- Three fabric place mats (two floral; one striped)
- Stapler and staples
- Pelmet board (1×3" board to fit inside the window)
- Two buttons
- Two premade curtain panels
- Two 2" metal L-brackets
- Tension rod to fit inside the window

Start to Finish

Cut the pelmet board to fit the inside of the window. Screw the L-brackets to the underside of the board, one at each end (see Diagram 1). Staple the striped place mat onto the pelmet board as shown in Diagram 2). Fold up the corners of the floral mats at the center and pin. Sew a button to each corner to hold it in place, and staple onto the pelmet board (see *Diagram 3*). Hang premade curtains in a coordinating fabric to complete the look.

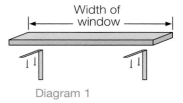

Width of window

Diagram 1

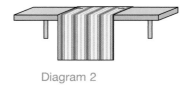

Diagram 2

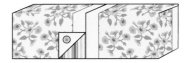

Diagram 3

French Rooster Chair Backs

Shown on pages 30–31

Supplies

- Cotton or cotton-blend curtains
- Cotton or cotton-blend fabric (for chairs)
- Delta Stencil Magic Stencil Paint Creme: Bark Brown #90-119, Barn Red #90-103, Black #90-112, Black Cherry #90-137, Garden Green #90-156, Garnet Red #90-124, Snow White #90-113, Sunflower Yellow #90-108, Warm Brown #90-120, Yellow Citron #90-107, Yellow Ochre #90-106
- Paintbrushes: ¼" and ½" stencil
- L.A. Stencilworks stencil: Poulet de Provence #405
- Stencil adhesive
- Masking tape

Start to Finish

Note: The basic instructions apply to stenciling fabric for curtains and chair backs or to stenciling walls. Prewash and press curtains or fabric before beginning to stencil. If stenciling a chair, center the stencil on the back. Use stencil adhesive to secure the stencils to the fabric or wall and mask off design elements as necessary.

Stencil the Hens: Stencil the hens with Yellow Ochre and Warm Brown, shading on the lower part of the body, neck, and tail. Stencil the wing area Snow White in the center, Warm Brown on the lower part, and Sunflower Yellow on the edge. Stencil the comb and waddle Black Cherry and the beak Sunflower Yellow. Apply Yellow Ochre to legs with Warm Brown shading next to the body. Stencil the cheek patches Warm Brown and the eyes Black.

Stencil the Roosters: Use a combination of Black, Garnet Red, and Yellow Ochre for the tail. Apply Yellow Ochre and Snow White to the wing, upper body, and face. Stencil the neck feathers Yellow Ochre and Snow White, with Barn Red shading where feathers join the face. Stencil the breast Garnet Red with Black shading. Complete the comb, waddle, beak, cheek patches, and legs as for the hen.

Finish the Design: Stencil the trees and grass Garden Green, Yellow Citron, and Bark Brown.

Bright and Sunny Bulletin Board

Shown on pages 32–33

Supplies

Refer to the Fabric Key *opposite right.*

- 1 yard of Fabric F
- ½ yard of Fabric C
- ¾ yard of Fabric D
- 24×36" piece of cotton batting
- 24×36" piece of acoustical ceiling tile
- Staple gun and staples
- 7½ yards of ½"-wide fusible interfacing
- Crafts glue
- 22×34" piece of white poster board
- Awl
- 5 feet of #1 picture wire (hangs pictures weighing up to 15 lbs.)
- Twenty-six ⅜"-diameter blue shirt buttons
- Six 1"-diameter orange buttons

The finished bulletin board measures 24×36 inches.

Start to Finish

Note: Quantities specified are for 54-inch-wide decorator fabrics. Additional yardage will be needed if using narrower fabric. Allow ½-inch seam allowances unless otherwise specified. The diagrams for this project are on page 128.

Cut the Fabrics: From Fabric F, cut a 34×46-inch background rectangle. From Fabric C, cut one pocket. From Fabric D, cut one pocket lining, four 1½×12-inch strips, and enough 1¼-inch bias strips to make 7½ yards when sewn end to end.

Sew the Fabrics: With right sides together, sew the Fabric C pocket piece and the Fabric D pocket lining together along the curved edge. Clip the curve and trim the seam to ¼ inch. Turn right side out; press, folding the scalloped edge of the lining to the front.

Place the pocket on the Fabric F background. Machine-baste through all three layers along the sides and bottom of the pocket.

To make pocket dividers, turn under and press ¼ inch along both long edges and one short edge of each 1½×12-inch Fabric D strip. With the pressed short edge at the top, pin the strips to the pockets as indicated on the diagram. Topstitch through all layers close to the pressed edges of each strip.

Assemble the Bulletin Board: On a smooth, flat surface, place Fabric F (with pocket attached) right side down. Center the batting on the Fabric F. Lay the ceiling tile, with white side down, on top of the batting. Fold the top, sides, and bottom edges to the back, diagonally folding and trimming the corners. Temporarily secure with pins. Check to see if the pockets are squarely placed on the tile; staple the fabric in place.

Fold and press the edges of the 1¼-inch strip, with wrong sides together, to form a ⅝-inch double-fold strip. Fuse the double-fold strip together using the fusible interfacing. Cut the strips to length and arrange them diagonally in a grid across the bulletin board front; tuck the ends into the pocket openings and wrap the remaining ends around the sides and top; pin at each intersection of the strips.

Generously apply glue to one side of the poster board; center and place it on the back of the tile. Weight the back with heavy books to keep the poster board flat; allow the glue to dry.

Pierce the back of the tile and one layer of the strip with the awl (see the Bulletin Board Diagram on *page 128* for placement). Thread wire through the holes, tighten the wire, and secure the ends by twisting them.

Glue small buttons at each point where small strips intersect. Sew large buttons to pockets.

Bright and Sunny Table Runner
Shown on pages 32–33

Supplies
Refer to the Fabric Key *below.*
- ½ yard of Fabric A
- ½ yard of Fabric D
- ⅜ yard of Fabric E
- 45×60" piece of cotton batting
- Thread to match fabrics
- Tailor's chalk or erasable fabric marking pen
- 3¾ yards of ¼"-diameter cording

The finished table runner is 14¼×51¾ inches.

Fabric Key
Fabric A: Floral plaid, Waverly "Pastoral"
Fabric B: Yellow plaid, Waverly "Playful"
Fabric C: Green stripe fabric
Fabric D: Watercolor print fabric
Fabric E: Blue/yellow print, Cyrus Clark "Jacey"
Fabric F: Floral, Waverly "Second Spring"

Start to Finish
Note: Quantities specified are for 54-inch-wide decorator fabrics. Additional yardage will be needed if using narrower fabric. All seam allowances are ½" unless otherwise specified.

Cut the Fabrics: From Fabric A, cut a 15¼×52¾-inch rectangle. From Fabric D, cut a 15¼×52¾-inch rectangle. From Fabric E, cut enough 1¾-inch wide bias strips to make 3¾ yards when sewn end to end. From the cotton batting, cut a 15¼×52¾-inch rectangle.

Shape the Runner: See the Table Runner Cutting Guide on *page 128*. Fold the Fabric A rectangle in half lengthwise and then crosswise. With the tailor's chalk or an erasable fabric marking pen, draw rounded corners using the cutting guide; cut on the drawn line. Place the batting on the wrong side of the Fabric D rectangle, aligning the edges. Unfold and layer the Fabric A piece on top of the batting, aligning all of the straight edges. Trim the Fabric D piece and the batting to match the Fabric A piece. Set all three pieces aside until needed.

Make the Piping: Sew the 1¾-inch fabric E bias strips with diagonal seams to make one continuous strip (see Making a Bias Strip, *page 128*). Trim the excess fabric, leaving ¼-inch seam allowances. Press the seam allowances open. With the wrong sides facing, fold the strip in half lengthwise and finger-press. Open the strip and align the cording along the fold. Refold with raw edges together. Use a cording or zipper foot to stitch close to the cording.

Assemble the Runner: Starting at one long edge of the Fabric A piece, pin the piping to the outer edges, aligning the raw edges and clipping to the seam line at curves. For a neat finish at the point where the ends overlap, cut the covered piping off 2 inches beyond the meeting point. Remove stitches between the cut edge and the meeting point. Clip the cording at the meeting point. Trim the unstitched fabric diagonally and fold this cut edge under ¼ inch. Pin in place. Machine-baste around the runner, following the stitching line of the piping.

Baste the batting to the wrong side of the Fabric D piece ½ inch from the raw edges. With the right sides together, sew Fabric A to Fabric D, using the row of basting stitches as a guide and leaving an opening for turning on one side. Turn and press. Slip-stitch the opening closed.

Bright and Sunny Chair Cover

Shown on pages 32–33

Supplies

Refer to the Fabric Key on *page 97*.

- 2½ to 3 yards of muslin
- Fabric marking pen
- 20×20" piece of 1¼" polyurethane foam
- Graph paper (optional)
- 1 yard of Fabric A
- 1½ yards of Fabric B
- 1 to 1½ yards of Fabric D
- ½ yard of Fabric E and F
- 7 to 8 yards of ¼"-diameter cording
- Threads to match fabrics
- Hook-and-loop tape
- One 1"-diameter orange button

View of Chair Cover Back

Start to Finish

Note: Quantities specified are for 54-inch-wide decorator fabrics. Exact amounts needed will vary, depending on the chair being covered. Pattern Pieces for the Chair Cover are on page 127. *Follow the directions below to calculate exact yardages. All seam allowances are ½-inch unless otherwise specified.*

Make a Muslin Pattern: Kitchen chairs come in a wide variety of sizes and styles. Study the style of the chair. Sometimes, it's a good idea to simplify or eliminate details to improve the look and fit of the chair cover. To ensure that the chair cover fits well, make a pattern by pin-fitting muslin to the chair.

Measure the length and width of the chair back; cut two pieces of muslin, each 4 inches larger than the measurements. With the fabric marker, label one piece "front" and one "back" (they may each have a unique shape). Locate and mark the lengthwise and crosswise grain (running parallel and perpendicular to the selvage edge, respectively) in the center of each piece.

Keeping the crosswise grains horizontal and the lengthwise grains vertical on the front and back, pin the two pieces of muslin together on the chair; drape the fabric smoothly and pin it to fit. Allow a little ease for multiple fabric layers and seam bulk.

When the muslin is pinned all the way around the back, try to slip the cover off the chair, trying not to tug or pull the fabric. Adjust the pins until the cover can be removed easily but fits snugly. Use the marker to draw a bottom for the chair back. Remove the muslin from the chair and mark the position of each pin on both the front and back. Remove the pins, smooth the lines, and add a ½-inch seam allowance; set aside.

Trace two triangle patterns from the pattern on *page 127* onto muslin or tissue paper. Pin them to the sides of the chair back pattern. They should overlap in the center 1½ to 2 inches. For a narrower chair, trim the outside edges equally. For a wider chair, add width to the outside edges equally. It may also be necessary to narrow the top and bottom angles to fit.

Measure the chair seat and cut a piece of muslin 4 inches larger than the measurements. Label it "seat" and mark the grain lines as before. Place the muslin on the chair seat and trace an outline. If there are vertical supports between the uprights, draw the outline in front of them. Add notches to indicate both edges of each side; these are guides for positioning the ruffle and the tabs securing the seat to the chair. Add a ½-inch seam allowance.

For the 2¼-inch boxing strip length, trace the seat

bottom shape without seam allowances onto polyurethane foam; cut out using a bread knife (an electric carving knife works especially well). Measure the circumference of the polyurethane foam and add 1 inch for ½-inch seam allowances.

For the 14-inch ruffle length, double the boxing strip length. If the back of the chair has upright supports, omit the ruffle in that area. Subtract the appropriate measurement before doubling the length of the boxing strip.

If desired, sketch the approximate measurements of each piece onto graph paper to determine the exact yardage needed for each fabric.

Cut the Fabrics: From Fabric A, cut the ruffle and two 2×7-inch tab rectangles. From Fabric B, cut one chair seat bottom, one chair back lining, one chair front lining, and two triangle linings. From Fabric D, cut one chair seat top, one chair back, one chair front, and a 2¼-inch-wide boxing strip. From Fabric E, cut enough 1¾-inch-wide bias strips to make 7 to 8 yards when sewn end to end. From Fabric F, cut two triangle-shape pieces.

Make the Piping: Join the 1¾-inch Fabric E strips with diagonal seams to make one continuous strip (see Making a Bias Strip Diagrams on page 128). Trim the excess fabric, leaving ¼-inch seam allowances. Press the seam allowances open. Fold the strip in half lengthwise with the wrong sides together and finger-press. Open the strip and align the cording along the fold. Refold with the raw edges together. Use a cording or zipper foot to stitch close to the cording.

Assemble the Cover:
Starting at one long edge of the Fabric D chair seat top, pin the piping to the outer edges, aligning raw edges and clipping into the seam line at the curves. Cut off the covered piping 2 inches beyond the meeting point. Remove the stitches between the cut edge and the meeting point. Clip the cording at the meeting point. Trim the unstitched fabric diagonally and fold under ¼ inch along that cut edge. Pin in place. Machine-baste around the piece on the stitching line.

With right sides together, stitch the short edges of the boxing strip together. Pin the boxing strip, right sides facing, to the Fabric D seat top; sew all the way around, using the machine basting as a guide. Machine-baste piping around the bottom edge of the boxing strip as directed above.

If more than one length is required for the ruffle, sew the short ends together to make a continuous piece. Fold the Fabric A ruffle in half lengthwise with wrong sides facing; fold and pin a ½-inch pleat about every 2 inches along the lengthwise raw edge of the ruffle. With raw edges matching, pin the

pleated ruffle loosely to the bottom piped edge of the boxing strip, leaving space for the uprights and vertical supports on the chair back.

Cut the ruffle strip to fit between the uprights at the chair back. Adjust the width and spacing of the pleats as needed. Unpin the ruffle from the boxing strip and hem the ends. Repin the ruffle to the boxing strip; then pin the boxing strip to the Fabric B seat bottom. Carefully sew around the seat bottom, leaving a 6-inch opening at the back for turning. Clip the seams, turn right side out, and press. Insert the foam seat shape. Slip-stitch the opening closed. Place the seat on the chair.

With the right sides together, sew the long edges of each tab together. Turn right side out and press. Finish the ends by serging, zigzag stitching, or turning in ½ inch and slip-stitching the opening closed. Attach the loop side of a 2-inch piece of hook-and-loop tape to each end of each tab. Place a tab around each upright support to determine the position for the hook end; attach it to the ruffle.

Machine-baste piping around the two equal edges of each triangle piece. With right sides together, sew one triangle piece to each triangle lining along the piped edges. Turn right side out and press.

Machine-baste the piping to the outer edge of the

Fabric D chair front piece. Also, machine-baste the piping to the bottom edge of the chair back piece. Baste both triangles to the right side of the chair back piece. With right sides together, stitch the chair back piece and chair front piece together along the outer edge, leaving the bottom edge open.

With the right sides together, stitch the outer edge of the chair back lining to the chair front lining, leaving an opening for turning on one side; do not turn. Slip the chair back/front piece into the back/front lining piece so right sides are together. Align the side seams. Sew all the way around the bottom. Turn right side out through the opening in the lining and press. Slip-stitch the opening closed. Overlap the triangles and sew a button through all layers of the back (see photo, *page 98*).

Bright and Sunny Lamp Shade
Shown on page 32

Supplies
Refer to the Fabric Key on *page 97*.
- ⅜ yard of Fabric A and C
- 3×6×5" self-adhesive lamp shade kit
- Crafts glue
- ⅝ yard of ½" wide trim, optional

Start to Finish
Note: Quantities specified are for 54-inch-wide decorator fabrics.

Cut the Fabrics: From Fabric A, cut one lamp shade piece using the Lamp Shade Diagram *left,* or the protective sheet from the kit, and adding a 1-inch seam allowance.

Cover the Lamp Shade: Center the wrong side of the Fabric A lamp shade piece on the sticky side of the shade. Press and smooth the fabric onto the shade. Trim any excess fabric on the opposite end to ½ inch. Fold the raw edge under and glue it to the shade.

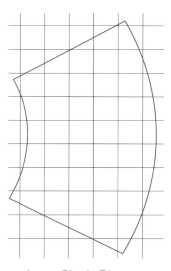

Lamp Shade Diagram

Clip the excess fabric at the top and bottom of the shade every inch, then turn it down and glue it to the inside of the shade.

Trim the Lamp Shade: From Fabric C, cut and sew enough 1¾-inch-wide bias strips to equal 1 yard when sewn end to end (see Making a Bias Strip and Binding Diagram 1, *page 128*). Join the strips with diagonal seams to make one continuous strip. Trim the seam allowances leaving ½ inch. Press the seam allowances open, then fold ¼ inch of fabric (long raw edges) on both sides of the bias strip and press (right-side-out) to meet in the lengthwise center. Working with 2 inches at a time, glue the bias strip over the top and bottom inside edges of the lamp shade, covering the raw edges of Fabric A and providing a neat finish on the inside.

Glue the braid trim to the top and bottom edges, overlapping the trim at the back seam of Fabric A.

Bright and Sunny Button-Back Curtains
Shown on page 32

Supplies
Refer to the Fabric Key on *page 97*.
- 37" piece of 1×3" lumber
- Two 2½" metal L-brackets
- 1⅞ yards of Fabric D (for face)
- 1⅞ yards of Fabric F (for lining)
- Two 1"-diameter orange buttons
- Thread to match fabrics
- Staple gun and staples
- Two 3×3×1" wooden blocks and finishing nails

Start to Finish
Note: The materials listed are for the curtain panels shown, which are 62 inches long and fit a window 35 inches wide. Specific measurements for this size are in parentheses. Quantities specified are for 54-inch-wide decorator fabrics. Additional yardage will be needed if using narrower fabric. All seam allowances are ½-inch unless otherwise specified.

Paint the mounting board to match the window trim or staple on lining fabric to cover it. For accurate measuring, temporarily install the mounting board on the wall. Firmly screw the L-brackets to the ends of the mounting board. Position the mounting board at the top of the window just above the window frame or molding (see Diagram 1, *below*). Screw it into the wall just enough to hold in position because it must be taken down again before completing the installation.

Determine the Width of Each Panel: Each panel should be half the width of the mounting board plus the depth (also called the return). Add 2 inches for seam allowances and an overlap (23½ inches).

Determine the panel length by measuring from the top of the mounting board to the desired bottom edge of the curtain. Add the depth of the mounting board and a ½-inch seam allowance (65½ inches). Cut two pieces of Fabric D (face) and Fabric F (lining) to the exact length and width desired.

Sew the Panels: Pin Fabric D (face) and Fabric F (lining) right sides together in pairs. Stitch side and bottom edges of each panel pair together, leaving the top edge open. Trim the corners and turn each panel right side out. Press carefully. Make sure both panels are precisely squared and even.

Assemble the Panels: At the window, remeasure the finished length from the

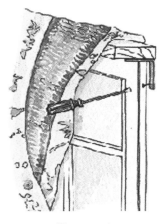

Diagram 1   Diagram 2   Diagram 3

desired bottom of the curtain to the top of the mounting board. Beginning at the bottom of each panel, measure and mark the length completely across the top.

Remove the mounting board from the wall. Align the panel length marking with the front edge of the mounting board. Staple the panel to the top of the board, starting at the return and making a diagonal fold to form a corner (see Diagram 2, *opposite*). Overlap the panels about 1 inch at the center. Fold the fabric back and firmly remount the L-brackets to the wall.

Fold panels back on each side; adjust to ensure that each side drapes evenly. Secure each panel in place with a button (see Diagram 3, *opposite*). To maintain the shape of the curtain panels at the sides, cut two blocks the depth of the mounting board from 1×3-inch lumber; paint them to match the window frame. Screw the blocks to the inside of the window frame, level with the buttons. Staple or thumbtack each panel to the block.

Executive Post Chair
Shown on pages 34–35

Supplies
Refer to the Fabric Key *below*.
- Fabric A for cushion top and small covered buttons
- Fabric B for cushion bottom
- Fabric C for gusset, loops, and large covered buttons
- Fabric D for covered piping
- Tracing paper and pencil
- 2" thick upholstery foam and serrated knife, utility knife, or electric knife
- Batting
- Upholstery spray adhesive
- Two yards of ¼"-diameter cotton welt
- Eight ⅝"-diameter covered buttons
- Two 1⅛"-diameter covered buttons
- Upholstery needle and thread

Fabric Key
Fabric A: yellow with white dot
Fabric B: white with yellow dot
Fabric C: stripe
Fabric D: blue with white dot

Start to Finish
Note: *All measurements include ½-inch seam allowances unless otherwise noted.* Using tracing paper and a pencil, trace the chair-seat shape. Using a serrated knife, utility knife, or electric knife, cut one shape from the upholstery foam for the cushion. Wrap the foam with batting and secure it with upholstery spray adhesive. Adding a ¼-inch seam allowance around the foam shape, cut the cushion top from Fabric A and the cushion bottom from Fabric B.

To figure the length for the gusset, measure the distance around the cushion and add ½ inch for each seam allowance. From Fabric C, cut a 3-inch-wide strip to this length for the gusset. With right sides together and the raw edges aligned, pin together the short ends of the gusset to make a continuous loop. Stitch the ends together. Press the seam open.

Make the Piping: Determine the length of piping needed by multiplying the length of the gusset by two. Cut the welt to the correct length. Referring to the diagrams for Making a Bias Strip on *page 128* for making covered piping, cut enough 1½-inch-wide bias strips from Fabric D to cover the cotton welt; using a zipper foot, sew the strips around the cord.

Cut the length of piping in half and pin it to the right side of the loop along one edge, aligning raw edges (begin the piping away from the seam to minimize the bulk in the seam allowances). Where the piping meets, overlap the ends 1 inch and cut the excess. Remove the stitching from the fabric cover in each end. Unfold the fabric and cut the ends of the cord to meet. Refold one end of the cover under the cord. On the remaining end, turn the cover under ½ inch and refold the fabric around the cord, concealing the raw ends of the fabric cover. Using a zipper foot and a long stitch length, baste the piping to the gusset loop. Baste the remainder of the piping to the other raw edge of the loop in the same manner.

Assemble the Cushion: With right sides together and the raw edges aligned, pin the gusset to the bottom cushion panel, centering the seam on the gusset at the center back of the panel. Using a zipper foot, stitch the bottom panel to the gusset following the previous line of basting for the covered piping. Clip the corners as necessary. Sew the top cushion panel to the gusset in the same manner, leaving an opening for inserting the batting-wrapped cushion.

Turn the cover right side out and press. Place the batting-wrapped cushion inside the cover and slip-stitch the opening closed.

Add the Details: Follow the manufacturer's instructions to assemble four ⅝-inch-diameter covered buttons with Fabric A and four buttons with Fabric B. Using a fine-tip marking pen and referring to the photograph on *page 35,* mark the placement of the four covered buttons on the top of the cushion. Referring to the Tufting Diagram on *page 128,* use a doubled length of upholstery thread and an upholstery needle to attach the buttons to the top and bottom of the chair cushion.

For tabs, cut two 4×6¾-inch strips from Fabric C. Fold each strip in half lengthwise with right sides together and raw edges aligned. Sew along the long side and one short side of each strip, leaving one short side open; trim the corners. Turn the strips right side out through the openings; press. Center and stitch a 1¼-inch-long buttonhole ½ inch from the finished edge of each strip. Topstitch the short open sides closed.

Place the cushion on the chair and mark the positioning of the ties on the sides of the cushion. Remove the cushion and hand-sew the ties to the sides. Cover two 1⅛-inch-diameter covered buttons with Fabric C and position the buttons to correspond with the buttonholes. Hand-sew the buttons to the cushion with a doubled length of upholstery thread.

Executive Post Lumbar Pillow
Shown on pages 34–35

Supplies
Refer to the Fabric Key on *page 101.*
- 1 yard of Fabric D
- 1½ yards of ¼"-diameter cotton welt
- Needle and coordinating thread
- Polyester fiberfill

The finished pillow measures 16½×7 inches.

Start to Finish
Note: All measurements include ½-inch seam allowances unless otherwise noted. From Fabric D, cut two 17½×8-inch rectangles for the pillow front and back. Referring to the instructions for Making a Bias Strip on *page 128,* cut enough 1½-inch-wide bias strips to make 1½ yards. Cover the cotton welt and sew the strips around the cord as shown to make one continuous length.

Beginning at the center of one long edge, pin the piping to the right side of one panel, aligning the raw edges. Where the piping

meets, overlap the ends one inch and cut off the excess. Remove the stitching from each end of the fabric cover. Unfold the fabric and cut the ends of the cord to meet. Refold one cover end under the cord. On the remaining end, turn the cover under ½ inch and refold the fabric around the cord, concealing the raw ends of the fabric cover. Using a zipper foot and a long stitch length, baste the welting to the front panel; pivot the stitching at the corners.

With right sides together and raw edges aligned, pin the front panel to the back panel. Using a zipper foot and a normal stitch length, stitch the back to the front along the basting line; pivot the stitching at the corners. Leave a long opening in one side for turning. Clip the corners. Press the seam.

Turn the cover right side out, pushing out the corners. Press the seam. Firmly stuff the pillow with polyester fiberfill, paying special attention to the corners. Slip-stitch the opening closed.

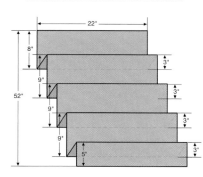

Pocket Board Diagram

Pocket Board
Shown on pages 34–35

Supplies
Refer to the Fabric Key on *page 101.*
- 18×24" piece of ⅜"-thick plywood
- 18×24" piece of ½"-thick foam
- ¾ yard of batting
- Spray adhesive
- ¾ yard of Fabric D
- Water-soluble marking pen
- Eight ⅝"-diameter covered buttons
- Needle and thread
- Staple gun and staples
- Two large picture-hanging rings

The finished board measures 18×24 inches.

Start to Finish
Make the Pockets: From Fabric D, cut a 22×52-inch rectangle. Starting at one 22-inch side and referring to the Diagram at *left,* fold four rows of pockets; press. Topstitch along the bottom of each pocket. With a 2-inch seam allowance, topstitch around all four edges of the fabric. Measure 6 inches from each side seam; mark lines extra to

make a twelve-square grid. Topstitch the lines to create twelve pockets.

Cover eight ⅝-inch-diameter buttons with Fabric D. Sew buttons at intersections of top pocket folds and vertical grid lines.

Assemble the Board: Using spray adhesive, glue foam to the plywood. Cut a 22×54-inch rectangle from batting; wrap it around the foam-covered plywood and staple it to the back.

Wrap the sewn pocket panel around the board, positioning the outside seams at the edges; staple the edges to the back. Measure and mark two points 3 inches from the top and 3 inches from each side of the board; attach picture hanging rings at the marks.

Mustard-Dyed Curtains
Shown on page 36

Supplies
- White or light-color natural-fiber curtains
- Yellow mustard in a squeeze bottle
- Red paste food coloring
- White vinegar

Start to Finish
Note: This process works best on 100-percent cotton, silk, or wool fabrics. Before dyeing the curtains, wash and dry the fabric to remove any sizing that would act as a barrier between the fabric and mustard. Iron fabric and tape it tautly to a paper-covered work surface.

Use yellow mustard in a squeeze bottle that squirts out a slender line. For better contrast, darken the mustard by adding a small bit of red paste food coloring to the container. Shake mustard and apply it in a pattern directly onto the fabric. Let the mustard set for 30 minutes until it's nearly dry. Rinse with a spray of warm water until the mustard is dislodged and water runs clear.

Note: There are two ways to set color: heat and chemical. Heat-setting is usually done by ironing, but can sometimes be done in the microwave. Clothes dryers do not get hot enough to set a dye. For chemical-setting, add white vinegar to the dye bath. To be safe, use both methods.

Immerse fabric in 10 quarts of warm water and 1 cup of vinegar, agitating it to remove the excess mustard. Seal wet fabric inside a microwave-safe plastic bag and heat on 50-percent power for 5 minutes, watching carefully so it doesn't scorch. Line-dry the fabric and press with an iron to further set the design.

Towel Shades
Shown on page 37

Supplies
- Linen dishtowels
- ½"-diameter curtain rings
- Shade-and-blind cord
- Two screw eyes
- 1×2" board
- ¼" dowel
- Small metal cleat

Start to Finish
Measure the window. Make shades long enough by overlapping and sewing the narrow hems on the short sides of the towels.

Stitch ½-inch plastic curtain rings to the long, hemmed edges on the wrong side of the towels. (Sew the first curtain ring 7 inches from the top of the towel, and the last curtain ring 2 to 5 inches from the bottom hem. Space the rings about every five inches, making sure both sides are even (see Towel Shade Assembly *right*.)

Cut a 1×2-inch board and a ¼-inch dowel the width of the window. Slide dowel through bottom rings and glue ends to towel. Staple top of the shade to the 2-inch side of the board.

On the other side, twist small screw eyes in line with the side rings.

Cut a piece of shade-and-blind cord for each row of rings. Cut one cord to double the length of the shade; the other cord should be that length plus the width. Determine on which side the string control will be; tie the short cord to the bottom ring on this side. Tie the longer cord to the other bottom rings. Secure with fabric glue. Run each cord through the rings directly above it and through both of the screw eyes at the top (both strings come out of the same eye). Trim the cord ends evenly.

Screw the 2-inch side of the board to the upper window frame. Screw a small cleat to the side of the window. To raise the shade, pull the cords and loop them around the cleat.

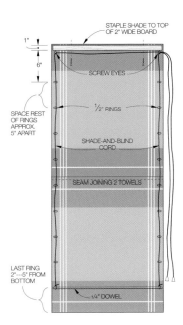

Towel Shade Assembly

Duvet Cover
Shown on pages 43–44

Supplies
Refer to the Fabric Key *below* and Determining Yardage, *opposite*.
- Fabric A for cover top
- Fabric B for cover reverse
- ¼ yard of Fabric C for flap band
- Cording with insertion header in determined yardage
- Nine 1⅛"-diameter buttons
- Fusible interfacing

The finished duvet cover measures 87×95 inches and fits a queen-size comforter.

Fabric Key
Fabric A: Cream-with-red toile
Fabric B: Gingham check
Fabric C: Red-with-cream toile
Fabric D: Cream-with-red vines
Fabric E: Red tone-on-tone stripe
(All fabrics are 54/55" wide.)

Start to Finish

Note: All measurements include ½-inch seam allowances unless otherwise noted. For the top, cut a full fabric panel width in the determined length. This will be the center panel unless the comforter is less than 53 inches wide. Cut the remaining fabric panel in half lengthwise. Trim the selvages from each panel.

Piece the Top: With right sides facing and raw edges aligned, pin one of the half panels to each side of the full panel, matching the print along the seam line; sew the panels together to make the top.

Even off the side panels to exactly match the length of the center panel. Round the two lower corners. Press the seams open and trim the side panels evenly to the determined width.

Piece the Bottom: For the bottom of the cover, cut and piece the fabric as for the front, but add an additional 30 inches in length. Cut the extra 30 inches off; set it aside for the facing and overlap on the front and the back.

Cut the 30-inch length into thirds across the width of the pieced panels. Each strip should measure 10 inches by the finished width of the cover. (Two strips will be used for the banded overlap and the remaining strip for the bottom cover facing.) Cut and piece a 6-inch strip of the band fabric to the cover width.

Cut and fuse interfacing to the wrong side of the band.

Assemble the Duvet Cover: With the raw edges aligned, use a zipper foot to sew the cording to the right side of the top, overlapping the ends at the center of the lower edge.

Make the Overlap: With the right sides facing and the raw edges aligned, make the banded overlap by sewing the long edges of the band strip to the overlap strips as shown in Diagram 1, *right.* Press the assembled strip in half with the wrong sides together as shown in Diagram 2. Beginning at the center, mark nine evenly spaced large buttonholes across the width of the overlap band and parallel with the edge, as shown in Diagram 2. Stitch the buttonholes.

With the right sides facing and the raw edges aligned, pin the overlap to the upper edge of the top on the right side. Sew the long edge and baste the side edges as shown in Diagram 3.

For the reverse facing, finish one long edge of the facing strip. With the raw edges aligned, sew the facing to the upper edge of the cover. Fold and press it to the wrong side and baste the side edges in place as shown in Diagram 4.

With the right sides facing and the side and lower edges aligned, pin the top and bottom together. The upper edge of the bottom should be just below the upper edge seam line of the top. Sew the side and lower edges together. Clip the corners, turn right side out, and press.

Turn the overlap at the upper edge to the other side and press. Sew buttons in place.

1

2

3

4

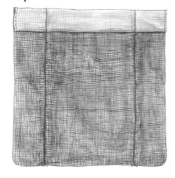

Duvet Cover
Assembly Diagrams

Determining Yardage

Duvet Cover

1. Finished size: (Width = desired width + 1" seam allowances. Length = desired length + 1" seam allowances.)
2. Number of fabric widths needed: (Number of fabric widths = cut width ÷ fabric width [round up to a whole width] + 1" seam allowances for piecing.)
3. Yardage needed for the top: (Yardage for the top = number of widths × length ÷ 36 inches; round up to the nearest half yard.) For fabric with a print to be matched, measure the print repeat and add the extra length to the total yardage. (Example: Cut size for the queen-size 87×95" cover shown is 88×96". 88"÷54" = 2 widths. 2×96" = 192"÷36"= 5½ yards. Add 1 yard to allow for the repeat = 6½ yards of fabric was needed for the cover top shown.)
4. Yardage needed for the bottom: Add ⅔ yard to the amount of fabric needed for the top to allow for the flap overlap.
5. Yardage needed for the cording: (Yardage = perimeter of the duvet cover cut dimensions + 4" for overlap.) Cut the cording. (Example: 88×2 = 176"; 96×2 = 192"; 176" + 192"=362" perimeter + 4" overlap = 366" (or 10¼ yards needed.)

Bed Skirt

1. Cut length: (Length = [side of bed × 4] + [end of bed × 2]).
2. Cut depth: (Depth = measurement from the top of the box springs to ½" from the floor + 1½" for seam and hem allowances.)
3. Number of fabric widths needed: (Cut length divided by the fabric width + 1" for each seam allowance.)
4. Total yardage needed: (Yardage = number of fabric widths needed × cut depth ÷ 36".) (Example: The cut dimensions of the featured bed skirt are 440×15½". 440"÷54" = 8.14 + 8" for seam allowances; round up to 8½ widths. 8½×15½" = 127½" = 3.54 yards, (or round up to 3⅔ yards of fabric needed.)

Bed Skirt
Shown on page 44

Supplies
Refer to the Fabric Key on *opposite* page and Determining Yardage, *left*.
- Fabric B for skirt
- Cotton sheet to fit box springs (for deck)
- Shirring tape (enough yardage to equal the sides and one end of the bed)

The finished bed skirt measures 60×80×14 inches and fits a queen-size bed.

Start to Finish
Note: All measurements include a ½-inch seam allowance unless otherwise noted.

Cutting and Piecing: Cut the determined number of widths from the fabric for the bed skirt (each will equal the cut depth). With right sides facing and the raw edges aligned, sew the short ends together. Press the seam allowances open.

Press under and sew a doubled ½-inch hem along one long edge. Sew shirring tape to the wrong side of the remaining long edge, being careful not to stitch into the cords. Knot the cords together at one end. Pull the cords from the other end to gather the fabric evenly to the appropriate length. Tie the ends of the cords together.

Measure the length and width of the box spring, and add 1 inch to each measurement. Cut the sheet to this measurement for the deck.

Beginning at one corner of the deck, sew the skirt to the deck along the sides and one end as shown in the Bed Skirt Assembly Diagram, *below*. Press the seam allowances toward the deck.

Along the upper edge of the deck and the skirt ends, turn under, press, and topstitch a ½-inch hem.

Bed Skirt Assembly Diagram

Pillow Shams
Shown on pages 44-45

Supplies
Refer to the Fabric Key
on *page 104.*
For two pillow shams:
- ⅔ yard of Fabric C for
  center fronts (allow extra
  to center motifs)
- 1¼ yards of Fabric B for
  borders and back
- 1½ yards of 45"-wide
  fleece
- 8 yards of braid with
  fringe

*Each of the finished
pillow shams measures
25½×31½ inches and fits
a standard or a queen-
size pillow.*

Start to Finish
*Note: All measurements
include ½-inch seam
allowances unless
otherwise noted.*
For Each Sham: From the
appropriate fabrics, cut one
20½×26½-inch panel for
the center front, centering
the print motif if desired; cut
two 19½×26½-inch panels
for the back; cut two
4×32½-inch strips for the
upper and lower borders;
and cut two 4×26½-inch
strips for the side borders.

From the fleece, cut one
26½×32½-inch panel.
To make the sham front,
sew the border strips to
the center panel edges,
mitering the corners (see
page 109 for instructions on
mitering corners). Clip the
center panel corners and
press. Baste the fleece panel
to the wrong side of the front.
For the sham back, turn
under and topstitch a
doubled ½-inch hem along
one 26½-inch edge of each
panel, hemming the right
edge of one panel and the
left edge of the other.
With right sides facing, pin
the backs to the front,
aligning the raw edges and
overlapping the hemmed
edges. Sew each pair
together along the outer
edges as shown in the
Pillow Sham Assembly
Diagram, *below.*
On the front, pin the
layers together along the
border. Stitch in the ditch
along the border/center
panel seam line.
For Trim: Baste the braid
along the edges of the
front. Turn the braid under
and overlap the ends at the
center of the lower edge.
Topstitch the braid in place
along both edges.

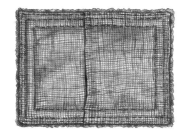

**Pillow Sham
Assembly Diagram**

Oversized Pillows
Shown on page 45

Supplies
Refer to the Fabric Key
on *page 104.*
- Fabric in yardage equal
  to twice the pillow form
  height, plus 1"
- Pillow form in size of
  choice
- Insertion trim equal to
  perimeter of pillow form,
  plus 1"

Start to Finish
*Note: All measurements
include ½-inch seam
allowances unless
otherwise noted.* From
the fabric, cut two panels
equal to the pillow form
measurements, plus 1 inch
for seam allowances.
Baste the insertion trim
along the edges of one
panel right side, aligning the
trim header edge with the
fabric raw edge. Turn under
and overlap the trim ends at
the center of one edge.
With right sides facing
and raw edges aligned, sew
the panels together, leaving
an opening for the pillow

form. Turn the cover right
side out; then press the
opening seam allowances
under. Insert the pillow
form and slip-stitch the
opening closed.

Envelope Pillow
Shown on page 45

Supplies
Refer to the Fabric Key
on *page 104.*
- 18"-square pillow form
- Two 19" squares each of
  Fabric E and Fabric D for
  pillow and flap
- 2¼ yards of brush
  fringe for edge
- 1 yard of braid with
  tassels and beads
  for flap
- 8"-long tassel
- Self-adhesive, double-
  sided basting tape
- Fabric marking pen

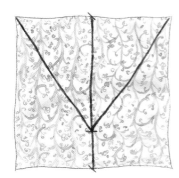

Envelope Pillow Diagram

Start to Finish

Note: All measurements include ½-inch seam allowances unless otherwise noted. Refer to the Envelope Pillow Diagram, *opposite* to mark the flap cutting lines on the wrong side of one flap square. Layer the flap squares with right sides together; cut the flap through both layers.

With right sides facing and raw edges aligned, sew the sides of the flap together. Clip the point and turn right side out. Press, and then baste the upper raw edges together. Tack the tassel loop to the flap point with the tassel top ½ inch from the point. Use basting tape to adhere the braid with tassels and beads along the flap sides; stitch close to each braid edge. With raw edges aligned, baste the flap right side up to the right side of one pillow panel.

Baste the brush fringe along the edge of the right side of the pillow front, overlapping the ends.

With right sides facing and raw edges aligned, sew the pillow panels together, leaving an opening for turning. Press the opening seam allowances under. Turn right side out, insert the pillow form, and slip-stitch the opening closed.

Bordered Motif Pillow
Shown on page 45

Supplies
Refer to the Fabric Key on *page 104*.
- 18"-square pillow form
- 11"-square of Fabric A (center the motif)
- Two 5×11" Fabric B strips for ends
- Two 5×19" Fabric C strips
- 19"-square of Fabric D for back
- 1¾ yards of ¾"-wide coordinating gimp trim
- 1¼ yards of coordinating cording with header
- Four 2"-long princess key tassels
- Four 1"-diameter chenille buttons
- Self-adhesive, double-sided basting tape

The finished pillow measures 18×18 inches square.

Start to Finish

Note: All measurements include ½-inch seam allowances unless otherwise noted. With right sides facing and raw edges aligned, sew one 5×11-inch Fabric B strip to each side of the center square. Press the seam allowances open. Sew one 5×19-inch Fabric C strip to the upper and lower edges. Press the seam allowances open.

Cut two 10-inch-long pieces of gimp trim for the center panel side seams. Cut two 19-inch-long pieces of gimp trim for the center panel upper and lower seams. Baste the trim to the center panel side seams, then to the upper and lower seams, covering the ends of the side seam trims. Topstitch in place close to each gimp edge. Sew a chenille button at each trim intersection.

With the tassels facing the inside of the front panel center and the tops ½ inch from the seam line, tack a tassel loop to each corner.

With the right sides facing and the raw edges aligned, baste the cording around the front panel edges, overlapping the ends at the lower edge center.

With the right sides facing and the raw edges aligned, sew the front and back panels together, leaving an opening for the pillow form. Press the opening seam allowances under. Insert the pillow form and slip-stitch the opening closed.

All Shirted Up Pillow
Shown on page 46

Supplies
- Six shirt fronts (for top)
- ½ yard of 60"-wide striped shirting fabric (for back and flange)
- Matching sewing thread
- 12×18" pillow form

The finished pillow measures 12X18 inches.

Start to Finish

Note: All measurements include ½-inch seam allowances unless otherwise indicated. Button shirt fronts together in unmatched pairs. Cut a 7×13-inch rectangle from each pair. From the striped shirting fabric, cut a 13×19-inch rectangle for the pillow back and enough 2-inch-wide strips to total 65 inches for the flange.

For Pillow Top: Sew together long edges on the three 7×13-inch rectangles. Sew short ends of the flange strips together. Press the strip in half lengthwise with wrong sides facing. Fold in ½ inch at one end of strip. Beginning at the bottom in the center with the folded end of the strip, pin the flange to the edges of the pillow top with the raw edges even. Trim the opposite end of the strip and fold ½ inch to meet at the center bottom. Baste.

Sew the pillow top and back together with right sides facing; turn right side out, and insert the pillow.

Sleek Retreat
Shown on page 60

Supplies
- Two towel rings with accompanying hardware
- Plastic wall plugs (if necessary)
- 8 to 9 yards of sheer fabric

Start to Finish
Measure the width of the bed and, using that measurement, mark two points on the ceiling above the headboard. Using plastic plugs if necessary, mount a towel ring on the ceiling at each of those points. Hem the ends of a length of sheer fabric (8 or 9 yards is necessary for most ceiling heights). Loop the fabric through the rings, letting the ends puddle on the floor.

Crowning Glory
Shown on page 48

Supplies
- Half-moon-shape metal corona
- Short, flat rod
- Extra-long, full-size flat sheet
- 54"-wide fabric
- Sewing thread to match

Start to Finish
Mount the metal corona to the wall 6 inches from the ceiling, centering it above the bed. To determine the length of all panels, measure from the top of the corona to the floor and add 9 inches. Cut all of the fabrics to this length.

Use an extra-long, full-size flat sheet for a soft backdrop. To make a channel for the top rod pocket, turn and press 2½ inches at the foot of the sheet toward the wrong side; sew close to the original edge. Hang on a short, flat rod between the ends of the corona.

For the Side Panels: Use 54-inch-wide fabric. To finish the side edges, turn

and press ½ inch toward the wrong side; then another 1½ inches. Sew close to the first fold. For the top rod pocket on the side panels, turn and press ½ inch toward the wrong side, then another 5 inches. Sew across the panel close to the first fold. Sew again 2 inches above the first line of stitching. Slide the panel onto the corona; mark the hem. Turn and press ½ inch toward the wrong side at the hem, then press again at the hem marking; sew in place. Repeat for the second panel. ***Note:** If you wish to line the panels in a different color fabric, cut two pieces of lining the same size as the side panels. Place one on each side panel with wrong sides together, treating them as one piece of fabric.*

Flower Shower Canopy and Bed Skirt
Shown on page 49

Supplies
- Fabric shower curtain
- Ceramic drawer pulls
- Flat sheet the size of the bed
- Tape measure and pencil
- 1×2" board, cut to shower curtain width
- Drill and drill bit
- Two large buttons

Start to Finish
Note: Before beginning, make sure the screw part of the drawer pulls will slip through the grommets or holes intended for shower curtain hooks.

Shower Curtain Canopy: Starting ½ inch from the floor, measure and mark the shower curtain height on the wall.

Measure the distance between the grommets or holes along the top edge of the shower curtain. Mark and drill holes for the drawer pulls into the board at these intervals. (For a narrow bed, use a shorter board and space the drawer pulls closer together for a gathered look.) Partially screw the drawer pulls into the board from the back, and attach the board to the wall. Beginning at one end, remove the drawer pulls, slip the shower curtain over the hardware, and replace the pulls. The shower curtain should cover the board.

Bed Skirt: Purchase a flat sheet the same size as the bed, coordinating the sheet color with the shower curtain. Remove the mattress from the bed and drape the sheet over the box spring. Position the sheet with the top hem at the headboard and the other edges brushing the floor, hemming the sheet if necessary. Pin an inverted pleat at each bottom corner. Sew on a large button to hold each pleat.

Soft and Sweet Blanket
Shown on page 54

Supplies
- 1¼ yards of 54–60"-wide mint green fleece
- Two packages of 2"-wide mint green satin blanket binding
- White thread
- Dark mint green rayon machine-embroidery thread
- Machine-embroidery needle
- Iron-on tear-away stabilizer
- Water-soluble stabilizer
- Water-soluble marking pen

The finished blanket size is 45 inches square.

Start to Finish
From mint green fleece, cut a 45-inch square. Cut four 48-inch strips from the blanket binding. If working with prefolded binding, work with the more narrow side facing up. Pin one strip of binding to encase one edge of the fleece, matching the crease down the center of the binding with the edge of the fleece. Sew together, beginning and ending the seam ¼ inch from the corners of the fleece (see Diagram 1, *below right).* Allow excess binding to extend beyond the edges. Repeat with remaining binding strips. Press the seam allowances toward the binding strips.

Overlap the binding strips at each corner (see Diagram 2). Align the edge of a 90° right triangle with the raw edge of a top binding strip so the long edge of the triangle intersects the seam in the corner. With a marking pen, draw along the edge of the triangle from the seam out to the raw edge. Place the bottom binding strip on top; repeat the marking process.

With the right sides of adjacent border strips together, match the marked seam lines and pin (see Diagram 3*).*

Beginning with a backstitch at the inside corner, stitch exactly on the marked lines to the outside edges of the border strips. Check the right side of the corner to see that it lies flat. Then trim the excess fabric, leaving a ¼-inch seam allowance. Press the seam open. Mark and sew the remaining corners in the same manner.

Choose a decorative machine-embroidery stitch to cover the stitched binding edge. Using dark mint green rayon machine embroidery thread, machine-embroider around the stitched edge of the blanket binding.

Sew the Monogram:
Choose a monogram style that is available for the sewing machine; program the monogram, following the manual. Practice on a scrap piece of fleece before monogramming the blanket. Cut pieces of tear-away and water-soluble stabilizers that are ½ inch larger all around than the expected monogram height and width. Iron the tear-away stabilizer to the back of the fleece. Pin the water-soluble stabilizer to the front of the fleece, directly above the tear-away stabilizer. Stitching from the front side of the fleece, sew the monogram. Tear both stabilizers away.

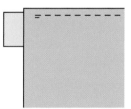

Diagram 1

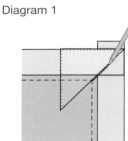

Diagram 2

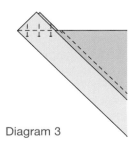

Diagram 3

Mitering Diagram

Fancy Border Animal-Print

Shown on pages 56-57

Supplies
- Blanket
- ⅓ yard bronze satin
- ½ yard animal print fabric
- ¼ yard coordinating animal print fabric
- 7 yards 1"-wide decorator ribbon
- Nineteen 1¼" covered buttons
- Ruler
- Matching thread for piecing
- Matching thread for quilting

Start to Finish

Note: Use a ¼-inch seam allowance unless otherwise indicated. Fabrics used were 54 to 58 inches wide. Before starting, measure the blanket width and divide that measurement in half to get the total number of strip sets needed.

Make the Checkerboard Edging: Using a rotary cutter and a mat will be the easiest way to cut the strips. Cut four 2½" × fabric-width satin strips, four 2½" × fabric-width strips in one print, four

4½"× fabric-width strips in the other print, and twenty 3-inch strips of decorative ribbon.

With right sides together, align the long sides of one satin strip and one print strip, and sew to create a strip set. Press the seam toward the print strip. Do the same with the remaining two strips. Using a rotary cutter and mat, cut the strip sets into forty-one 2½-inch segments, as shown in Diagram 1, *below*. Sew the segments right sides together, so they create a checkerboard row, as shown in Diagram 2. Press all seams in the same direction.

Add the Ribbon Edgings: Cut two strips of ribbon the length of the checkerboard strip. Fold one of the ribbon strips in half lengthwise. Pin the folded ribbon strip to the upper edge of the checkerboard row with the raw edges aligned and sew. The folded ribbon edge should extend ¼ inch beyond the checkerboard. Repeat for the lower edge of the checkerboard.

Fold the twenty 3 inch pieces of ribbon into triangular shapes, often called Prairie Points, as shown in the Ribbon Prairie Point Diagram, *below*. Pin the Prairie Points on alternating squares, right sides together, along the lower edge of the checkerboard. Sew the Prairie Points in place.

Sew the Backing: Sew the two 4½-inch-wide animal print strips together to create a strip slightly wider than the blanket. Fold the lower edge under ¼ inch and press. Sew the upper edge of the backing fabric to the upper edge of the checkerboard row, right sides together. *Note: The ribbon edging should be tucked inside. Be sure that it does not get caught in the seam.*

Attach the Edging: Draw a chalk line 4¼ inches from the upper edge of the blanket. Lay the prairie point side of the checkerboard row face down along the chalk line and pin in place so that when it is flipped back the ribbon edge will be along the top edge of the blanket. *Note: The seam will be inside the blanket edging.*

Sew the seam, being careful to avoid the Prairie Points. With right sides together, pin the short sides of the checkerboard row and the backing fabric together and sew so that when turned right side out, the edge of the blanket is encased. Slip-stitch to close.

Using coordinating thread and a walking foot, quilt diagonal lines through all the squares. Cover the nineteen buttons, following the manufacturer's directions; sew one at the intersection of every other square.

Animal Print Trim Diagram

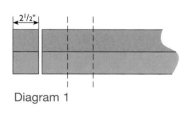

Diagram 1

Diagram 2

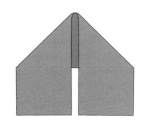

Ribbon Prairie Point Diagram

Fancy Border Brocade-Edge
Shown on page 56

Supplies
- Blanket
- ½ yard black/gold brocade fabric
- ½ yard black velvet
- 3 yards bullion fringe
- Matching thread for piecing
- Matching thread for quilting
- Ruler
- Chalk pencil

Start to Finish
Note: Use a ¼"-seam allowance unless otherwise indicated. Fabrics used were 54 to 58 inches wide.

Cut and Assemble the Fabric: Using a rotary cutter and a mat will be the easiest way to cut the strips. Cut two 8" × fabric width velvet strips and two 6½" × fabric-width brocade strips. Sew the black velvet strips together with right sides facing to form one long strip; trim to 1 inch longer than the width of the blanket. Fold the strip lengthwise, right sides facing, and sew the ends

shut. Turn right side out. Pin the long raw edges together and baste. Pin the bullion fringe to the basted line; sew it in place.

Sew the brocade strips, right sides together, to make a continuous strip the width of the blanket plus 1 inch. Fold one lengthwise side of the strip under ¼ inch and press. Center the opposite, unfolded side of the brocade strip on the fringe/flap with right sides together, and sew along the long cut edge.

Attach the Trim: Draw a chalk line 2 inches down from the top of the blanket. With the brocade and fringe/flap pieces still right sides together, pin the seamed edge to the chalk line and sew it to the blanket. The fringe/flap piece will hang free below the brocade.

Fold the brocade strip in half lengthwise, mark the width of the blanket on it, and sew the short ends shut. Trim the seam and turn the casing over the top of the blanket. On the underside of the blanket, slip-stitch the folded edge of the brocade strip to the blanket.

Using the chalk pencil and ruler, mark a 45-degree quilting line every 2 inches. Quilt along the chalk lines with black thread and a walking foot.

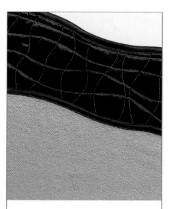

Fancy Border Wavy-Edge
Shown on page 56

Supplies
- Blanket
- 1 yard purple satin
- ¼ yard purple velvet
- Gold metallic thread
- Matching thread for piecing

Start to Finish
Note: Use a ¼-inch seam allowance unless otherwise indicated. Fabrics used were 54 to 58 inches wide.

Cut the Fabric: Using a rotary cutter and a mat will be the easiest way to cut the strips. Cut two 8" × fabric-width satin strips, two 6½ ×14" pieces of velvet, and five yards of 2¼" bias strips from satin (see Making A Bias Strip on page 128).

Attach the Wavy Trim: With right sides together, sew the short raw edges of the purple satin. Fold the satin strip lengthwise and cut an irregular curving line into the long raw edge. Pin the satin strip to the blanket, matching the curves to the top edge

of the blanket. Pin securely into place. With a walking foot and gold metallic thread, quilt irregular wavy lines in a loose checkerboard pattern. Trim the top edge of the blanket along the wavy edge of the satin.

Finish with Bias Tape: To make bias tape, fold the 2¼-inch bias strips in half and press; fold in half again and press. Pin the bias tape over the bottom long raw edge. Topstitch with gold metallic thread along both edges of the bias trim. Bind the raw edges on the sides and top of the blanket with bias tape, mitering the corners, and topstitch with gold metallic thread.

Make the Bows: Sew the short raw edges of one 6½×14" piece of velvet, leaving a 2-inch opening in the seam. Fold the velvet so the seam is in the center, pin the top and bottom, and sew. Turn the velvet bows right side out.

Gather the center and wrap a 2½×3" piece of purple satin around to the back, tucking the raw edges under, and sew to secure. Tack the bows to the blanket at the beginning and end of the bias trim.

Fancy Border Log Cabin Block
Shown on page 56

Supplies
- Blanket
- ¼ yard brown fabric
- ¼ yard green fabric
- ¾ yard silver brocade fabric
- 2¾ yards braided piping
- Matching thread for piecing
- Matching thread for quilting

Start to Finish
Note: Use a ¼-inch seam allowance unless otherwise indicated. Fabrics used were 54 to 58 inches wide. Before starting, measure the blanket width and divide by eight to get the number of quilt blocks needed.

Cut the Fabric: From the brown fabric, cut:
  four 4½" squares
  four 1½x4½" strips
  four 1½x5½" strips
  four 1½x6½" strips
  four 1½x7½" strips
From the green fabric, cut:
  four 4½" squares
  six 1½x4½" strips
  six 1½x5½" strips
  six 1½x6½" strips
  six 1½x7½" strips
From the silver fabric, cut:
  two 4½" squares
  six 1½x4½" strips
  six 1½x5½" strips
  six 1½x6½" strips
  six 1½x7½" strips
From backing fabric, cut:
  two 8½x45" strips

Assemble the Quilt Blocks:
To make a quilt block, sew one 4½-inch square and one 1½x4½-inch strip on one side of the square, right sides together. Repeat for the opposite side. Press seams away from the center. Sew one 1½x5½-inch strip along the top raw edge, right sides together. Repeat for the bottom raw edge. Press seams away from the center.

Repeat this process for the remaining 6½-inch and 7½-inch strips, as shown in the Log Cabin Block Diagram, *below.* The quilt block should be 8½-inches square.

Make the number of blocks needed to reach across the width of your blanket; the full-size blanket shown on *page 56* required

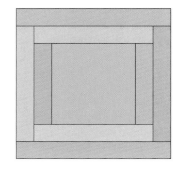

Log Cabin Block Diagram

10 blocks. Mix and match strips and squares. Sew the blocks together end to end and press all seams.

Finish the Trim: Align the braided piping with the sides and top raw edge of the quilt block strip. Using a zipper foot, sew the piping to the three sides. ***Note:*** *The piping is easier to work with if trimmed to a ¼-inch seam allowance.*

Sew the backing strips, right sides together, along the short raw edge to connect the two. Press the seam open. Pin the top and sides of the backing to the quilt block strip, right sides together. Using a zipper foot to get close to the piping, sew only the top edge.

Attach the Trim: Draw a chalk line 8¼ inches down from the top edge of the blanket. Pin the bottom of the quilt-block strip face down to the back of the blanket (when sewn and turned toward the front, the trim will enclose the seam and the piped edge will fall at the upper edge of the blanket). Sew in place.

Turn the piece toward the front of the blanket. With right sides together, pin the short raw edges together and stitch, using a zipper foot. Trim and turn right side out.

On the back of the blanket, turn up ¼ inch along the raw edge and slip-stitch. Using a walking foot and matching thread, quilt by stitching in the ditch around all squares.

Faux Four-Poster
Shown on page 61

Supplies
- Four circular finials with hardware to screw into the ceiling
- Four plastic plugs (if necessary)
- Drapery scarves or lengths of fabric
- Plumb line or a string with a weight

Start to Finish
Note: Unless it will screw into wood, each finial may require a plastic plug.
To determine the finial placement at each corner of the bed, tie a pencil or small weight to the end of a string or use a plumb line. Dangle the string from the ceiling so it clears each corner, allowing for the fabric fullness so it can skim the floor or fall into puddles; mark the spots on the ceiling. Attach the finials to the ceiling. Drape lengths of fabric through the finials to form a rectangle or cross in the center.

Tab-Top Valance
Shown on pages 64–65

Supplies
- Chenille fabric for valance
- Contrasting cotton fabric for valance border
- Matching sewing thread
- Assorted cotton fabric scraps for tabs
- Pencil
- Straight pins
- Large buttons

Start to Finish

Measure the window. Cut a chenille rectangle that is 1½ times the width and at least ¼ the depth of the window.

Cut a cotton strip that is 4½ inches wide and as long as the chenille rectangle. Aligning the long edges, place the right side of the cotton strip facing the wrong side of the chenille rectangle; sew together using a ¼-inch seam allowance. Press the seam allowance toward the cotton strip. Fold under and press ¼ inch on the long raw edge of the strip. With the wrong side inside, fold the strip in half lengthwise so the folded edge covers the seam. Topstitch the pressed edge. Press each side edge under ½ inch twice for hems; topstitch on each side.

Determine the desired number of 2-inch-wide tabs spaced 6 inches apart. For each tab, cut a 4½×10½-inch strip from one of the assorted cotton fabric scraps. Fold each strip in half lengthwise with the right sides inside. Using a ¼-inch seam allowance, sew the long edges together to form a tube. Press the seam allowances open, centering the seam on the tube.

Use the pencil to make a light mark on one end of each seam ¼ inch from the bottom edge; mark a point on each fold 1¼ inches

from the bottom edge. Form pointed tabs by sewing each tube at an angle from one fold mark to the seam mark, then back up to the opposite fold mark. Trim the seam allowances to ¼ inch. Turn the tabs right side out, pushing the point out completely with the pencil eraser, and press.

Fold under and press one inch along the top edge of the valance; then turn and press again for a hem. With the seam side facing up, slip the unfinished tab ends underneath the top hem, evenly spacing the tabs. Pin the tabs in place. Topstitch the top and bottom edges of the top hem, securing tabs in the stitching. Fold the tabs toward the front so the pointed ends evenly overlap the valance, pinning them in place. Sew a button on each point to attach it to the valance.

Friendly Frogs Bumper Pads
Shown on pages 66–67

Supplies
Refer to the Fabric Key on *page 114*.
- 1⅞ yards of Fabric A
- 1¾ yards of Fabric B
- 2½ yards of muslin
- 2½ yards of heirloom batting
- 2¼ yards of 24"-wide high-density batting
- 1¾ yards of ¾"-wide white hook-and-loop tape
- ¼ yard of fusible webbing
- 4½×4" piece of Fabric C
- 4½×16" piece of Fabric D
- One square of lemon yellow felt
- Scrap of poster board
- Machine-embroidery needle
- Machine darning foot for free-motion stitching

Fabric Key

Fabric A: White tone-on-tone
Fabric B: Light green variegated
Fabric C: Pastel green flannel
Fabric D: Pastel plaid flannel
Fabric E: Pastel yellow dot
Fabric F: Yellow chenille
Fabric G: Yellow/purple plaid seersucker
Fabric H: Yellow plaid seersucker

Start to Finish

Note: The finished set of four bumper pads fits a standard baby crib. Each of the two end pieces measures 26½×9⅜ inches, and each of the two side pieces measures 51½×9⅜ inches. Because of variations in shrinkage, the finished sizes may vary.

The quantities specified are for 44/45-inch-wide cotton fabrics. All seam allowances are ¼ inch unless otherwise specified.

Cut the Fabric: From Fabric A, cut ten 4½×44-inch strips and two 4½×18-inch strips. Cut twenty 11×2½-inch strips for the ties. From Fabric B, cut ten 4½×44-inch strips and three 4½×18-inch strips. From both the muslin and heirloom batting, cut two 22×30-inch rectangles and two 22×54-inch rectangles.

Assemble the Patchwork: Sew the long edges of three 4½×44-inch Fabric B strips to two 4½×44-inch Fabric A strips, alternating the colors and starting with Fabric B to make a strip set. Press all seam allowances toward the darker color. Repeat to make a second pieced strip set. Cut each of the pieced strip sets into nine 4½×20½-inch segments (see Diagram 1, *below*).

Sew the long edges of three 4½×44-inch Fabric A strips to two 4½×44-inch Fabric B strips, alternating the colors and starting with Fabric A. Press all seam allowances toward the darker color. Repeat to make a second pieced strip set. Cut each of the pieced strip sets into nine 4½×20½-inch segments (see Diagram 2).

Sew the long edges of three 4½×18-inch Fabric B strips to two 4½×18-inch Fabric A strips, alternating the colors and starting with Fabric B. Press all seam allowances toward the darker color. Cut the pieced strip set into four 4½×20½-inch segments (see Diagram 3).

Make the Bumper Pads: Referring to the Bumper Pads Assembly Diagram, *opposite*, lay out segments to make two ends and two sides.

Sew the long edges of the segments together, matching the seams, to make two 28½×20½-inch rectangles for the ends and two 52½×20½-inch rectangles for the sides.

Add the Details: Apply fusible webbing to the back of the print and plaid flannel fabrics. Transfer the frog body and belly patterns, *opposite*, onto poster board and cut out the pieces. Trace four frogs onto the fused side of the plaid flannel and four bellies onto the fused side of the print flannel; cut them out. Peel away the backing and fuse the pieces in place as shown in the Bumper Pads Assembly Diagram, *opposite*.

Using a machine blanket stitch and coordinating rayon machine embroidery thread, machine-embroider around the edges of the frogs and bellies to attach them to the bumper sections. Cut two ovals from lemon yellow felt for each frog. Zigzag-stitch the ovals to the head and embroider an eyeball on each oval. Machine-embroider the mouth with a narrow satin stitch. Using a long backstitch, machine-embroider the hopping lines as shown in the Bumper Pads Assembly Diagram.

Quilt the Bumper Pads: Place one piece of muslin on the work surface. Matching the sizes, layer a piece of batting over muslin; then place the corresponding pieced section on top with the right side facing up (the batting should be slightly larger than the pieced section). Pin the three layers together with straight pins.

Change the sewing machine foot to the darning foot and lower the feed dogs. Beginning at the frog, free-motion-stitch around the frog and the hopping lines, echoing the shapes.

Working outward from this point, quilt the remainder of the bumper in a meandering

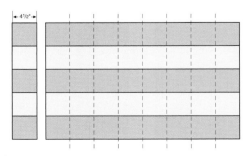

Diagram 1-Cutting the Strips

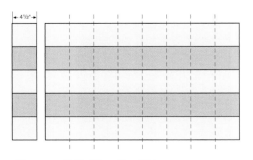

Diagram 2-Cutting the Strips

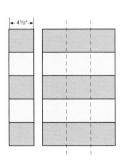

Diagram 3 Cutting the Strips

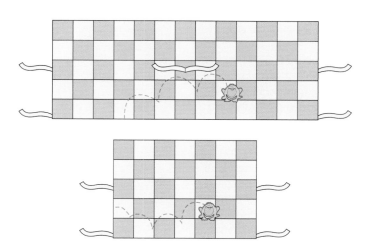

Bumper Pads Assembly Diagram

Bumper Pad Frog Pattern

fashion. Zigzag-stitch around the raw edges of each patchwork section. Repeat for each bumper pad section.

Machine wash and dry the quilted bumper sections to shrink the batting and create an "aged" texture.

Make the Ties: Fold lengthwise and press the raw edges of one 11×2½-inch tie strip under ½ inch to the wrong side. With right sides out, fold and press the strip in half again, matching the long edges. Topstitch the ties closed along the three open sides. Repeat to make 20 stitched tie strips.

Cut a 3-inch length from the loop half of the tape; sew to one tie end. Cut a 1¼-inch piece from the hook half of the tape; sew to the opposite end of the tie (it should also be on the opposite side of the tie). Repeat with each tie. Fold each tie in half 5½ inches from the end with the loop half of the tape.

Trim away the excess muslin and batting from each bumper. Referring to the Bumper Pads Assembly Diagrams, *above,* pin the folded edge of each tie along the raw edges of each end bumper and at the center of each side bumper. With wrong sides facing out and long edges aligned, fold each bumper in half.

Sew the three open edges, leaving a 10-inch opening along the long edge of the end bumpers and two 10-inch openings along the long edge near the middle of each half portion. Clip the bulk from the corners, press the seam open, and turn each panel right side out.

Sew through the middle of the side bumpers to create two chambers for the batting. Cut a piece of high-density batting to fit inside each panel; slip batting into panels through openings. Machine-stitch the openings closed.

Tailored Crib Skirt
Shown on pages 64–65

Supplies
Refer to the Fabric Key *opposite.*
- 3½ yards of Fabric A
- ⅞ yard of Fabric D
- ⅝ yard of Fabric E
- 6¼ yards of white pom-pom fringe
- 6¼ yards of white rickrack trim
- Water-soluble marking pen

The finished crib skirt fits a standard-size crib.

Start to Finish
Note: Quantities specified are for 44/45-inch-wide cotton fabrics. All seam allowances are ½ inch unless otherwise specified.

Cut the Fabric: From Fabric E, cut a 53¾×27¾-inch rectangle for the deck. Cut two 36¾×11-inch strips across the grain for the skirt ends. With right sides facing and short raw edges aligned, sew the fabric lengths together. Press the seam allowance open. Trim the pieced strip to measure 70½×11inches for one skirt side. Repeat to make one more 70½×11-inch strip for the opposite skirt side.

From Fabric D, cut two 36¾×4-inch strips across the grain for the skirt ends. With right sides facing and short raw edges aligned, sew the fabric lengths together. Press the seam allowance open. Trim the pieced strip to measure 70½×4 inches for one skirt side. Repeat to make one more 70½×4-inch strip for the opposite skirt side.

From Fabric A, cut two 36¾×3-inch strips across the grain for the skirt ends. With right sides facing and short raw edges aligned, sew the fabric lengths together. Press the seam allowance open. Trim the pieced strip to measure 70½×4 inches for one skirt side. Repeat to make one more 70½×4-inch strip for the opposite skirt side.

Sew the Skirt Ends: With right sides facing and raw edges aligned, sew the pom-pom fringe to one long edge of one Fabric E skirt end strip. With right sides facing and raw edges aligned, sew one long edge of the Fabric D skirt end strip to the pom-pom fringe edge of the Fabric E skirt end strip. Overcast the seam with a zigzag stitch. Press the seam allowance toward the plaid fabric.

With right sides facing and raw edges aligned, sew one long edge of the Fabric A skirt end strip to the remaining long edge of the Fabric D skirt end strip. Overcast the seam as before and press the seam allowance toward the Fabric A strip.

Turn under and press each side edge ¾ inch to the wrong side. Fold ¾ inch under on each edge again and press. Sew close to the inner folded edge to hem the skirt end sides.

Turn under and press the bottom edge ½ inch to the wrong side. Fold the pressed edge under so the pressed edge meets the Fabric D strip/Fabric A strip seam. Pin from the wrong side so the pressed-under edge slightly covers the seam. With right side facing up, hem the bottom folded edge just to the left of the seam. Remove pins while stitching. Sew rickrack trim over the Fabric D/Fabric A strip seam. Repeat to make an additional skirt end.

Using the marking pen, measure and mark 4 inches inward from each short hemmed edge on the skirt end. With wrong sides facing, fold and press the fabric on the mark. With right side facing up, bring the folded edge over to meet the short-hemmed edge, forming half of a box pleat as shown in the Crib Skirt Assembly Diagram, *below.* Press the pleat well and pin the top edge of the pleat along the unfinished edge.

Sew the Skirt Sides: Make two skirt sides as for skirt ends, substituting skirt side strips in place of skirt end strips.

Aligning the short edges, fold one skirt side in half to find the center; mark with the marking pen. Measure and mark 4 inches to either side of the center mark. With wrong sides facing, fold and press the fabric on the side marks. Bring each folded edge inward to meet the center mark, forming a box pleat as shown in the Crib Skirt Assembly Diagram, *below.* Press the pleat well and pin the top edge of the pleat in place along the raw edge. Measure and pleat the ends of each skirt side with a half-pleat, as for the skirt ends.

Assemble the Crib Skirt: Refer to the Crib Skirt Assembly Diagram, *below.* With right sides facing and raw edges aligned, sew the skirt ends to the deck along the short edges. Sew the skirt sides to the deck along the long edges. Press the seam allowances toward the deck. Topstitch the deck close to the seam.

Top of the Morning Curtain Valance
Shown on pages 67 and 69

Supplies
Refer to the Fabric Key on *page 114.*
- Fabric A
- Fabric D
- Fabric E
- White pom-pom fringe
- White rickrack trim
- Water-soluble marking pen or pencil

The double-fullness curtain valance shown measures 15 inches long with a 2-inch stand-up ruffle and a 1½-inch-wide rod pocket.

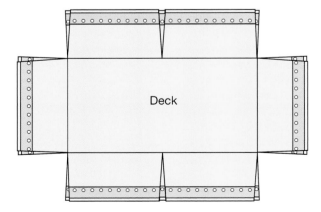

Deck

Crib Skirt Assembly Diagram

Start to Finish

Note: Determine the size to cut the valance fabrics. (Length = desired finished length + 1½-inch bottom hem + 4-inch top hem. Width = desired finished width × 2 [for double fullness] + 1 inch for the seam allowances.) Quantities specified are for 44/45-inch-wide cotton fabrics. All of the seam allowances are ½ inch unless otherwise specified.

From Fabric E, cut enough 15½-inch-wide strips to achieve the calculated valance width. With the right sides facing and the short raw edges aligned, sew the fabric lengths together. From Fabric A, cut enough 3-inch-wide strips to achieve the calculated valance width. With right sides facing and short raw edges aligned, sew the fabric lengths together. Press all seam allowances open.

With right sides facing and raw edges aligned, sew the pom-pom fringe to one long edge of the Fabric E strip. With right sides facing and raw edges aligned, sew one long edge of the Fabric D strip to the pom-pom fringe edge of the Fabric E strip. Overcast the seam with a zigzag stitch. Press the seam allowance toward the plaid fabric.

With right sides facing and raw edges aligned, sew one long edge of the Fabric A strip to the remaining long edge of the Fabric D strip.

Overcast the seam as before and press the seam allowance toward the Fabric A strip.

Turn and press each side edge under ¾ inch to the wrong side. Fold each edge under again ¾ inch and press. Sew close to the inner folded edge to hem the valance sides.

Turn under and press the bottom edge ½ inch to the wrong side. Fold the pressed edge under so it meets the Fabric D/Fabric A strip seam. Pin from the wrong side so the pressed-under edge slightly covers the seam. With right side facing up, hem the bottom folded edge just to the left of the seam, removing the pins while stitching. Sew rickrack trim over the Fabric D/Fabric A strip seam.

Using the marking pen, measure and mark a line 4 inches inside the top edge of the Fabric E strip. Turn and press the top edge to the wrong side along the mark. Place a piece of masking tape on the sewing machine, 2 inches to the right of the needle position. Position the pressed edge of the valance against the inner edge of the tape and sew a 2-inch hem. Turn under and press the remaining raw edge ½ inch, and sew close to the pressed-under edge, forming a rod pocket.

Pocket Helper
Shown on page 68

Supplies
Refer to the Fabric Key on page 114.
- 2½×44" rectangle of Fabric G
- ½ yard of Fabric F
- ⅝ yard of light green pom-pom fringe
- 6" length of ¾"-wide hook-and-loop tape

Start to Finish

Note: All of the seam allowances are ½ inch unless otherwise specified.
Enlarge the patterns on the inside back cover to the desired size. From Fabric F, cut two backs and one front, and two 16×3½-inch rectangles for the ties.

Topstitch the pom-pom fringe onto the right side of the curved front edge. Cut the 2½×44-inch Fabric G strip in half; with right sides facing, sew one long edge of the 2½×22-inch strip to the curved front edge. Press the seam allowance toward the strip. Fold under ½ inch on the remaining long edge of

the strip. Pin, then stitch the folded edge over the seam.

With wrong sides facing, fold the front along the box pleat lines as indicated on the pattern, with each fold toward the center. Pin along the bottom edge.

With right sides facing, pin the front to the back. Layer the right side of the second back piece against the wrong side of the front. Sew the side and bottom edges together. Press the seam allowances open. Turn the piece right side out, with wrong sides facing and the backs against each other.

Fold and press the raw edges of a 16×3½-inch tie strip under ½ inch to the wrong side. With the right sides facing out, fold and press the strip in half, matching the long edges. Topstitch the ties closed along the three open sides. Repeat to make a second stitched tie strip. With raw edges together, pin the ties to the outer layer of the back at the tie marks indicated on the pattern.

Using the remaining 2½×22-inch Fabric G strip, bind the back piece as for the front. Fold the side edges under, as well as the long edge. Fold the tie upward so it can be stitched to the bound edge of the outer back. Stitch the front to the back at the center front of the organizer, forming two pockets.

Cut two 1½-inch pieces from the hook half of the hook-and-loop tape. Sew to the inner-layer back on the tie marks 1½ inches down from the bound edge. Cut two 1½-inch pieces from the loop half of the hook-and-loop tape; sew to tie ends.

Shed Some Light Lamp Shade
Shown on pages 67 and 69

Supplies
Refer to the Fabric Key on *page 114*.
- Purchased lamp with truncated square lamp shade
- Scrap of fabric slightly larger than one side of the lamp shade
- ⅓ yard of Fabric H
- 2×44" strip of Fabric A
- 2 yards of light green pom-pom fringe
- Tracing paper and pencil
- Dark mint green rayon machine-embroidery thread
- Glue

Start to Finish
Note: All seam allowances are ½ inch. The shade cover has a slight ease in the fit. Using tracing paper and a pencil, trace one side of the lamp shade. Add 1 inch to the bottom edge. Allow an additional 2 inches on each side for box pleats. Add ½ inch to the top and side edges. Cut the pattern from scrap fabric. To make the box pleats, fold each side inward at the 2-inch mark to meet the raw side edge. Place the scrap side over one side of the shade.

If the fit is pleasing, proceed with making the actual shade cover from Fabric H. Cut four sides, using the pattern. With right sides facing and raw edges aligned, sew the four sides together to make a continuous loop. Using the Fabric A strip, and with right sides facing, sew one long edge of the strip to the bottom of the loop. Fold the remaining long edge of the strip under ½ inch; press. Pin the folded edge over the seam. Stitch in place.

Sew a decorative machine stitch along the center of the Fabric A strip using dark mint green rayon thread.

Box-pleat the fabric at the corners; baste-stitch in place. Slip the cover onto the shade. Glue the top edge of the cover to the top of the shade, wrapping and gluing the raw edge to the inside of the shade. Glue pom-pom fringe to the top edge of the shade cover.

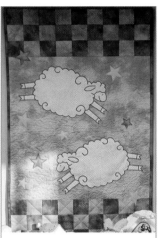

One Lamb, Two Lamb Wall Quilt
Shown on pages 70–71

Supplies
Refer to the Fabric Key *below*.
- 1⅛ yards of Fabric A
- ½ yard of Fabric B and C
- 12×16" piece of white-on-white print fabric
- 3×5" pieces of Fabric D, Fabric E, and Fabric F
- 24×37" piece of batting
- ½ yard of paper-backed fusible-adhesive material
- Matching sewing threads
- Rotary cutter and self-healing mat

The finished quilt measures 18½×31 inches.

Fabric Key
Fabric A: Hi Fashion Fabrics "Marble Mania," Robin's Egg
Fabric B: Hi Fashion Fabrics "Marble Mania," Seafoam
Fabric C: Hi Fashion Fabrics "Marble Mania," Lilac
Fabric D: Hi Fashion Fabrics "Marble Mania," Coral
Fabric E: Hi Fashion Fabrics "Marble Mania," Meringue
Fabric F: Hi Fashion Fabrics "Marble Mania," Peach

Start to Finish
Note: Quantities specified are for 44/45-inch-wide cotton fabrics. All seam allowances are ¼ inch unless otherwise specified. The appliqué pieces for this project are found on page 128. To make tracing onto fusible-adhesive material easy, they are printed in reverse.

Cut the Fabric: From Fabric A, cut one18½×19½-inch rectangle and one 24×37-inch rectangle. From Fabric B, cut three 2½×44-inch strips. From Fabric C, cut three 2½×44-inch strips and three 2¼×44-inch strips.

Make the Border: Stitch one 2½-inch Fabric C strip to each long edge of one 2½-inch Fabric B strip. Press the seams toward Fabric B; set aside. Sew the remaining 2½-inch Fabric B strips to the long edges of the remaining 2½-inch Fabric C strip. Press the seams toward Fabric C.

Use a rotary cutter, mat, and acrylic ruler to cut each pieced strip set into 2½×6½-inch segments (see Diagram 1, *opposite*).

For the top border, begin sewing segments together. Continue until there are nine segments in the strip. Press all seams in the same direction. Repeat with remaining segments for the bottom border.

Stitch the top and bottom borders to the short sides of the 18½×19½-inch Fabric A rectangle. Press the seams toward the borders.

Add the Appliqué Pieces:
Place the fusible-adhesive material, paper side up, over the appropriate appliqué pattern pieces. Trace five medium stars; following the manufacturer's instructions, fuse two to the wrong side of the Fabric D piece, two to the wrong side of the Fabric F piece, and one to the wrong side of Fabric E piece. Trace four small stars; fuse two to the wrong side of Fabric E, one to the wrong side of Fabric D, and one to the wrong side of Fabric F.

Trace one lamb, including all detail lines. Turn the pattern piece over and trace a second lamb. Fuse both lambs to the wrong side of the white-on-white print fabric.

Cut out all appliqué shapes. Place the lamb pieces, fabric side up, on a light table or tape against a window in daylight. Trace the detail lines lightly onto the fabric with a pencil. (These lines will be covered with satin stitching.)

Remove the paper backing from the appliqué pieces. Referring to the Wall Quilt photo, *opposite*, for instructions, arrange the

appliqués on the quilt. Note that a few stars overlap the border seam. When satisfied with the position of the appliqué pieces, follow the manufacturer's instructions to fuse them into place.

Add the Details: With wrong sides together, sandwich the batting between the appliquéd top and the 24×37-inch Fabric A rectangle. Baste through all layers. Using a narrow satin stitch, machine-appliqué around each star, covering all raw edges.

Using medium blue thread and a narrow satin stitch, machine-appliqué the outlines and all detail lines on the lambs. For the eye, take only three or four stitches, making sure to backstitch at the beginning and the end.

Finish the Project: Quilt the Fabric A sky, use matching thread. Attach a darning foot, lower the feed dogs on the machine, and stitch in a meandering "free-motion", avoiding the stars and lambs; see photo *below*.

Free-Motion Stitching

Use matching thread to quilt in the ditch (sew along the seam line) between the Fabric A center and the border. Quilt straight lines connecting opposite corners of each Fabric B square.

Join the 2¼-inch Fabric C strips with diagonal seams to make one continuous binding strip (see Diagram 1, *page 128*). Trim the excess fabric in the seam, leaving ¼-inch seam allowances. Press the seam allowances open. With the wrong sides together, fold the binding strip in half lengthwise; press.

Beginning in the center of one side, place the binding strip against the right side of the quilt top, aligning the raw edges of the binding strip with the raw edge of the quilt top. Fold over the beginning of the binding strip about ½ inch. Sew through all layers, stopping ¼ inch from the corner (see Diagram 2, *page 128*). Backstitch; clip the threads. Remove the quilt from beneath the presser foot.

Fold the binding strip upward (see Diagram 3, *page 128*), creating a diagonal fold, and finger-press. Holding the diagonal fold in place with your finger, bring the binding strip down in line with the next edge, making a horizontal fold that aligns with the top edge of the quilt (see Diagram 4, *page 128*).

Start sewing again at the top of the horizontal fold, stitching through all layers. Sew around the quilt, turning

each corner in the same manner. Upon returning to the starting point, lap the binding strip end over the beginning fold. Trim the batting and backing fabric even with the quilt top edges.

Turn the binding over the edge of the quilt to the back. Hand-stitch the binding to the backing fabric, making sure to cover any machine stitching. To make mitered corners on the back, hand-stitch the binding until reaching a corner; fold a miter in the binding and take a stitch or two in the fold to secure it. Then stitch the binding until reaching the next corner; finish the remaining corners in the same manner.

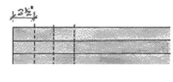

Diagram 1

Lamb Bumper Pads

Shown on pages 70–71

Supplies

Refer to the Fabric Key *on* page 118.

- ⅜ yard of Fabric A
- 2¼ yards of Fabric B
- 1 yard of Fabric C
- 12×16" piece of white-on-white print fabric
- 12" square of Fabric D
- 14" square of Fabric E
- 12" square of Fabric F
- 1 roll of Fairfield Bumper Batting
- 1¼ yards of paper-backed fusible-adhesive
- 11¼ yards of ¼"-diameter cording
- Matching sewing threads
- Medium blue thread
- Rotary cutter and self-healing mat
- Acrylic ruler

The set of four pads fits a standard baby crib. Each Checkerboard Pad measures 28×10 inches. Each Lamb Pad measures 52×10 inches.

Start to Finish

Note: Quantities specified are for 44/45-inch-wide cotton fabrics. All seam allowances are ¼ inch unless otherwise specified. The appliqué patterns for this project are found on page 128.

Cut the Fabric: From Fabric A, cut eight 10½×11-inch rectangles. From Fabric B, cut seven 2½×44-inch strips, two 52½×10½-inch rectangles, two 10½×28½-inch rectangles, and sixteen 1¼×22-inch strips. From Fabric C, cut eight 2½×44-inch strips and ten 1¼×44-inch strips.

Sew the Checkerboard Pads: Sew the long edges of three 2½×44-inch Fabric C strips to the long edges of two 2½×44-inch Fabric B strips, alternating the two colors and starting with Fabric C. Press all seams toward Fabric C.

Sew the long edges of three 2½×44-inch Fabric B strips to the long edges of two 2½×44-inch Fabric C strips in the same manner. Press all seams toward Fabric B. Cut each of the pieced strip sets into fourteen 2½×10½-inch segments (see Diagram 1, *right*). Divide the segments into sets, with seven of each of the color combinations in each set.

Sew the long edges of the segments together, matching the seams, to make two 10½×28½-inch rectangles. Press all seams in the same direction.

Cut the batting into two 10½×28½-inch pieces. Place each checkerboard bumper top over the batting and either zigzag-stitch or machine-baste ¼ inch from the raw edges.

Make the Piping: Join the 1¼-inch Fabric C strips with diagonal seams to make one continuous strip. Trim the excess fabric from the seams, leaving ¼-inch seam allowances. Press the seam allowances open. With the wrong sides together, fold the strip in half lengthwise and finger-press. Open the strip and align the cording along the fold. Refold with raw edges together. Use a cording or zipper foot to stitch close to the cording.

Pin piping to the outer edges of each bumper, aligning raw edges and clipping to the seam line at the corners. Set the unused piping aside for use in the Lamb Bumper Pads. For a neat point where the ends overlap, cut the covered piping off 2 inches beyond the meeting point. Remove the stitches between the

cut edge and the meeting point. Clip the cording at the meeting point. Trim the unstitched fabric diagonally and fold that cut edge under ¼ inch. Pin in place.

Assemble the Checkerboard Pads: For the ties, fold the 1¼×22-inch Fabric B strips in half lengthwise with the right sides together. Sew along the long edge of each strip using a ⅛-inch seam allowance. Turn right side out and press. Fold each strip in half crosswise; finger-press. Pin one strip diagonally across each corner of each bumper pad with the fold on the cording stitching line. Set the eight unused ties aside for use in the Lamb Bumper Pads. With a zipper foot, stitch around the top of the checkerboard along the piping stitching line. Fold both ends of each tie toward the center of the checkerboard top and pin them out of the way.

With right sides together, pin one of the 10½×28½-inch Fabric B rectangles to

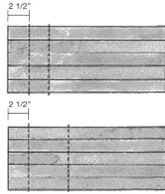

2 1/2"

2 1/2"

Diagram 1

each checkerboard top. Using the zipper foot, stitch around all sides, leaving a 4-inch opening for turning. Turn right side out, remove pins from ties; press. Slip-stitch opening closed with matching thread.

Using thread to match Fabric B, machine-quilt straight lines connecting the opposite corners of each Fabric B square (see Marking and Quilting Diagrams, *right*).

Sew the Lamb Pads: Stitch three 2½×44-inch Fabric C strips to the long edges of two of the 2½×44-inch Fabric B strips, alternating the two colors and starting with Fabric C. Press all seams toward Fabric C. Cut the new pieced strip set into ten 2½×10½-inch segments.

For each lamb bumper top, sew four 10½×11-inch Fabric A rectangles to five strip segments alternately; begin and end with a strip segment. Press seams toward the rectangles.

Add the Appliqué Pieces: Place the fusing-adhesive material, paper side up, over the appropriate appliqué pattern pieces.

Trace four large stars; fuse to the wrong side of the Fabric E square. Trace 14 medium stars; fuse eight to the wrong side of Fabric D and six to the wrong side of Fabric F. Trace 12 small stars; fuse ten to the wrong side of Fabric E and two to the wrong side of Fabric F.

Use the pattern to trace two lambs, including all detail lines. Turn the pattern over; trace two more lambs in the same manner. Following the manufacturer's instructions, fuse all lambs to the wrong side of the white-on-white fabric.

Cut out all appliqué shapes. Place the lamb pieces, fabric side up, on a light table or tape them against a window in daylight. Trace the details onto the fabric with a pencil. (The lines will be covered with satin stitching.)

Remove the paper backing from the appliqué pieces. Referring to the Bumper Pad Placement Diagram *below,* arrange the appliqués on the quilt. Note that a few stars overlap the border seam. When satisfied with the position of the appliqué pieces, follow the

manufacturer's instructions to fuse them into place.

Using matching thread and a narrow satin stitch, machine-appliqué around each star, covering all raw edges. Using medium blue thread and a narrow satin stitch, machine-appliqué the outlines and all detail lines on the lambs. For the eye, take only three or four stitches, making sure to backstitch at the beginning and the end.

Assemble the Lamb Pads: Cut the remaining bumper batting into two pieces that measure 10½×52½ inches. Lay each lamb top over the batting pieces and zigzag around the raw edges.

Pin and sew the piping and ties to the lamb tops in the same manner as for the checkerboard tops. With right sides together, pin one of the 10½×52½-inch Fabric B rectangles to each top. Using the zipper foot, stitch around all sides, leaving an opening for turning. Turn right side out, remove the pins and press. Slip-stitch the opening closed.

Using thread that matches Fabric A, machine-quilt around all stars and lambs, and ½ inch inside each

Fabric A square. Use thread matching Fabric B to quilt in the ditch (sew along the seam line) between the Fabric A squares and the checkerboard strips, and to machine quilt lines between opposite corners of each Fabric B square.

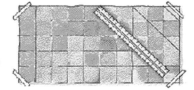

Marking Diagram

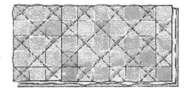

Quilting Diagram

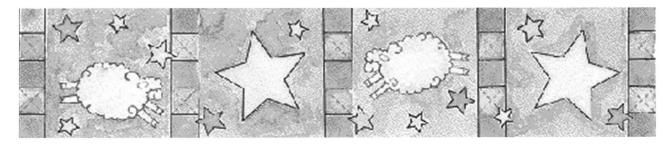

Bumper Pad Placement Diagram

Lamb Crib Pillow

Shown on pages 70–71

Supplies

Refer to the Fabric Key *on page 118.*

- ⅜ yard of Fabric A
- ⅛ yard of Fabric B
- ¼ yard of Fabric C
- 6×8" piece of white-on-white print fabric
- 3×5" piece of Fabric D
- 2×4" piece of Fabric E
- 3" square of Fabric F
- 8" square of paper-backed fusible-adhesive material
- 14×18" piece of lightweight cotton batting
- 14×18" piece of tear-away fabric stabilizer
- 1⅝ yards of ¼"-diameter cotton cording
- Matching sewing threads
- Medium blue thread
- Rotary cutter and self-healing mat
- Acrylic ruler
- 12×16" rectangular pillow form

The finished pillow measures 12×16 inches.

Start to Finish

Note: Quantities specified are for 44/45-inch-wide cotton fabrics. All seam allowances are ¼ inch unless otherwise specified. The appliqué patterns for this project are found on page 128. For easy tracing onto fusible-adhesive material, they are printed in reverse.

Cut the Fabric: From Fabric A, cut one 8½×12½-inch rectangle and two 10½×12½-inch rectangles. From Fabric B, cut twelve 2½-inch squares. From Fabric C, cut twelve 2½-inch squares and enough 1¼-inch wide strips to equal 60 inches when sewn end to end.

Sew the Pieces: For the left border strip, stitch four 2½-inch squares together, alternating colors (see the Piecing Diagram *below*). Press seams in the same direction. Stitch the border to the left short side of the 8½×12½-inch rectangle. Press the seam toward the border.

Noting the position of the top square in the left border, for the top border strip, sew seven squares together so the alternating color sequence continues at the

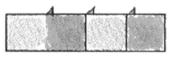

Piecing Diagram

corner. Sew the strip to the top edge of the left border and the Fabric A rectangle.

For the right border strip, sew five squares together, continuing the color alternation. Sew the strip to the right edge.

For the bottom border strip, sew eight squares together, alternating the colors in the same manner; stitch the border strip to the bottom of the rectangle.

Add the Appliqué Pieces: Place the fusible-adhesive material, paper side up, over the appropriate appliqué pattern pieces. Trace three medium stars; fuse two to the wrong side of the Fabric D piece and one to the wrong side of the Fabric F piece. Trace two small stars; fuse them to the wrong side of the Fabric E piece. Trace one lamb, including all detail lines; follow the manufacturer's instructions to fuse it to the wrong side of the white-on-white fabric.

Cut out all appliqué shapes. Place the lamb piece, fabric side up, on a light table or against a window in daylight. Trace the detail lines lightly onto the fabric with a pencil. (These lines will be covered with satin stitching.)

Remove the paper backing from the appliqué pieces. Referring to the Pillow Placement Diagram *below right*, arrange the appliqués on the pieced pillow top. Follow the manufacturer's instructions to fuse the applique pieces in place.

Note: A few stars will overlap the border seam.

With wrong sides together, sandwich the batting between the appliquéd top and the tear-away stabilizer. Baste through all layers. Using matching thread and a narrow satin stitch, machine-appliqué around each star, covering all raw edges.

Using medium blue thread and a narrow satin stitch, machine-appliqué the outlines and all detail lines on the lambs. For the eye, take only three or four stitches, making sure to backstitch at the beginning and the end.

Assemble the Pillow: Use matching thread to quilt in the ditch (sew along the seam line) between the pillow front and border, and quilt straight lines connecting the opposite corners of each Fabric B square. Remove the tear-away stabilizer.

For the Piping: Join the 1¼-inch Fabric C strips with diagonal seams to make one continuous strip. Trim the excess fabric in the seams, leaving ¼-inch seam allowances. Press the seam allowances open.

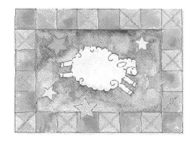

Pillow Placement Diagram

With the wrong sides together, fold the strip in half lengthwise and finger-press. Open the strip and align the cording along the fold. Refold with raw edges together. Use a cording or zipper foot to stitch close to the cording.

Pin the cording to the outer edges of the pillow top, aligning the raw edges and clipping to the seam line at the corners. For a neat point where the ends overlap, cut the covered piping off 2 inches beyond the meeting point. Remove the stitches between the cut edge and the meeting point. Clip the cording at the meeting point. Trim the unstitched fabric diagonally and fold that cut edge under ¼ inch, then pin in place.

Narrow-hem one 12½-inch edge of each 10½×12½-inch pillow back rectangle by pressing the raw edge under ¼ inch twice and topstitching near the first fold.

Lay the pillow top on a flat surface, right side up. Align the 12½-inch end with the raw edge of one of the pillow backs, placed right side down. In the same manner align the remaining pillow back with the other end. The hemmed edges overlap in the middle of the pillow. Pin the layers together.

Using the zipper foot, sew around the pillow. Clip the corners. Turn the pillow right side out through the back opening. Insert pillow form.

Lamb Window Valance
Shown on page 70

Supplies
Refer to the Fabric Key *on page 118.*
- ⅜ yard of Fabric A
- 1 yard of Fabric A
- ⅛ yard of Fabric B
- ⅛ yard of Fabric C
- 3×5" piece of Fabric D
- 3×5" piece of Fabric E
- 2×4" piece of Fabric F
- 8" square of paper-backed fusible-adhesive material
- Matching sewing threads
- Rotary cutter and self-healing mat
- Acrylic ruler
- Tailor's chalk

The finished valance measures 41×18 inches and will fit a window up to 38 inches wide.

Start to Finish
Note: Quantities specified are for 44/45-inch-wide cotton fabrics. All seam allowances are ¼ inch unless otherwise specified. The appliqué patterns for this project are found on page 128. To make tracing onto fusible-adhesive material easy, they are printed in reverse.

Cut the Fabric: From Fabric A, cut one 12½×42½-inch rectangle and one 22½×42½-inch rectangle. From Fabric B, cut ten 2½-inch squares. From Fabric C, cut eleven 2½-inch squares.

Piece the Fabric: Make a checkerboard strip by stitching the 2½-inch squares of Fabric B and Fabric C together alternately, beginning and ending with Fabric C squares. Stitch the 12½×42½-inch Fabric A rectangle to one long edge of the checkerboard border strip. Press all seams toward the checkerboard border.

Stitch the 22½×42½-inch Fabric A rectangle to the remaining long side of the checkerboard border strip. Press the seam toward the checkerboard border.

Fold the resulting 36½×42½-inch rectangle in half with right sides together to form an 18¼×42½-inch rectangle with the checkerboard strip parallel to the fold (bottom). Match the raw edges and pin. Along each short edge of the folded rectangle, measure 1¼ inch from the long raw edge (top) and make a line with tailor's chalk. Measure one inch below the first line and make a second line. (The space between the two lines is the opening for the curtain-rod casing.)

Starting at the bottom, sew along one short edge to the first casing line, backstitch, and cut the thread. Skipping over the casing space, backstitch and then stitch to within ¼ inch of the top. Turn the corner and sew the long edges together, stopping ¼ inch before coming to the second short edge.

Turn the corner and sew to the first casing line, backstitch, and cut the threads. Sew from the second marked casing line to about 3 inches from the fold, backstitch, and cut the thread. Turn through the opening and press. Slip-stitch the opening closed.

Add the Appliqué: Lay the fusible-adhesive material, paper side up, over the appliqué pattern pieces. Trace three medium stars; follow the manufacturer's instructions and fuse two to the wrong side of the Fabric D piece and one to the wrong side of the Fabric F piece. Trace five small stars; fuse them to the wrong side of the Fabric E piece.

Cut out all appliqué shapes and remove the paper backing from each one. Referring to the photo *top left,* arrange appliqués on the front of the valance. Note that a few stars will overlap the border seam. Fuse the stars.

Using sewing thread that matches each star and a satin stitch, machine-appliqué the stars in place, covering all raw edges.

Finish the Project: Use thread that matches Fabric B to quilt in the ditch (sew along the seam line) above and below the checkerboard row and to machine-quilt straight lines between opposite corners of each Fabric B square.

Cozy Comfort Rug
Shown on page 78

Supplies
- ½ yard each of eleven different 45–60"-wide cotton fabrics
- 1¼ yard of 45"-wide cotton fabric for backing
- Fabric marking pencil
- Rotary cutter and self-healing cutting mat

The finished rug measures 24×36 inches.

Start to Finish
Cut a 28×40-inch piece from the backing fabric. With the marking pencil on the wrong side of the backing, make dots every six inches to form a grid, leaving a 2-inch-wide margin on all sides (see the Chenille Throw Rug Diagram *above*).

Cut a total of 120 six-inch squares on the straight grain of the fabric; divide these into stacks of five, stacking each piece either randomly (photo step 1, *opposite*) or according to the order preferred. (Before starting the project,

make test patches with various combinations.)

Aligning the corners with the grid dots, pin four stacks to make a row across the 28-inch-wide side of the backing. Mark the bias of each square by measuring from corner to corner (photo step 2, *opposite*). Stitch through all six layers along these diagonal lines (see photo step 3, *opposite*). Using a zipper foot, stitch parallel rows every ⅝ inch to make channels covering the entire row of squares (see photo step 4, *opposite*). Using the cutting mat and a rotary cutter, cut through the top five layers along the center of each channel (see photo step 5, *opposite*).

Pin another row of four stacks on the backing, again using the grid dots as guides; mark a chevron pattern in the opposite direction (see the photo *above*), sew, and cut the channels as above. Continue adding rows of stacks, repeating the above steps to make six rows.

Finishing: Bind the outer edges by double-folding the backing toward the front, covering about ¼ inch along the outer edges of the patchwork; pin in place, mitering the corners.

Topstitch all of the edges. Machine-wash and dry the rug to create the chenille texture (see photo step 6, *opposite*). The more it is washed and dried, the fluffier the chenille will become.

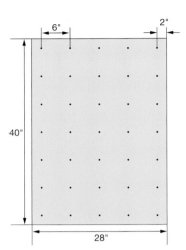

Chenille Throw Rug Diagram

Cozy Comfort Trimmed Towels and Wastebasket
Shown on page 78

Supplies
- Five 2"-wide strips of five different cotton fabrics
- 3½"-wide strip of backing fabric
- Cotton terrycloth towels
- Solid-color wastebasket
- Rotary cutter and self-healing cutting mat
- Hook-and-loop tape rounds
- Fabric glue
- Glue that adheres to surface of wastebasket

Start to Finish
Chenille Trim: Measure the width of the towel (or measure the distance around the wastebasket). Use this measurement to cut five 2-inch-wide pieces; stack the pieces right sides up. Cut one strip of backing fabric, adding 1½ inches to both the length and the width. Center the stack of five fabrics, with right sides up, on the background fabric; pin them together. Mark a 45-degree angle and stitch along the line; sew parallel rows of stitching every ⅝ inch to cover the entire piece. Cut through the top five layers between the rows of stitching. Double-fold the backing fabric to the front to cover the cut edges; topstitch through all layers. Machine-wash and dry the towel to create the chenille texture.

Towel: Pin strip to the towel; sew around the edges.

Wastebasket: Glue small rounds of hook-and-loop tape to the back of the strip (with fabric glue) and each side of the wastebasket (with a type of glue that adheres to its surface), aligning them to meet.

Chenille Trimmed Towel

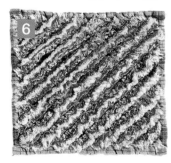

Chenille Step-by-Step

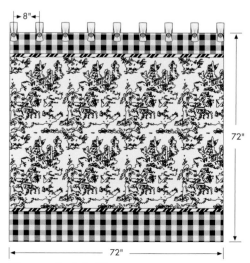

Shower Curtain Diagram

8"
72"
72"

Buttoned Border Shower Curtain
Shown on pages 76–77

Supplies
- 3½ yards toile fabric (to allow for matching)
- 2¼ yards check fabric
- 18"-square piece of ticking fabric
- 4 yards of cording for piping
- Ten buttons
- Thread to match fabric

Start to Finish

Note: This shower curtain measures 72 inches square. For a custom fit, measure the shower/tub opening and make adjustments as needed. Cut 12 feet of 1-inch-wide bias strips from the ticking and seam together at the ends (see Making a Bias Strip on *page 128*). Fold the cording into the center of the long strip and sew next to the cording using a zipper foot. Seam two pieces of toile, matching the pattern, to make a 74-inch-wide×53-inch-long panel (see the Shower Curtain photo, *left*). Sew the piping to the top and bottom of the panel. Cut one 15×74-inch strip from the check fabric and sew it to the bottom of the panel. Cut one 14×74-inch strip from the check fabric and fold it in half lengthwise, wrong sides together. Sew the raw edges to the top of the panel. Topstitch the top of the panel ¼ inch from the upper edge. Hem the panel sides by turning under ½ inch twice and pressing. Machine-stitch the sides. Hem the bottom of the panel by folding under ½ inch, then 2 inches, and pressing. Slip-stitch to make the hem.

To make the tabs, cut nine 6×9-inch pieces of check fabric. Fold one piece in half lengthwise and sew along all three sides, leaving a 2-inch-wide opening. Turn and press. Slip-stitch the opening closed. Repeat for all of the tabs. Pin the tabs equally along the top of the curtain and sew to the back. Fold the tab over the front of the panel and pinch it together (see photo *above left*). Machine-stitch through the pinched portion of each tab to hold it in place. Sew a button onto each tab.

Black 'n White Roman Shade
Shown on pages 76–77

Supplies
- Roman shade kit
- Toile fabric; see shade kit for amount
- Decorative trim
- Fabric glue

Start to Finish
Note: This shade was mounted above the window casing.
Measure the window opening carefully and note the measurements before purchasing materials. Using the toile fabric, follow the manufacturer's instructions for making the shade. Attach the trim to the lower edge of the shade with fabric glue and let dry. Install the shade.

Skirt the Issue
Shown on pages 79 and 83

Supplies
- Drapery fabric (or other fabric that drapes well)
- Light -to medium-weight drapery-lining fabric
- ¼-inch-diameter decorative cording
- Measuring tape
- Matching sewing thread
- Monofilament (fishing line)
- Hook-and-loop tape with one adhesive-back side and one sewable side, such as Velcro brand Half & Half
- T-pins

Start to Finish
Measure the sink perimeter, subtracting the width of the plumbing in back. Multiply the perimeter measurement by 2½ for proper fullness; add ½-inch seam allowances for each side. Measure from the floor to the bottom of the sink, adding ½-inch hem and seam allowances. Use these measurements to cut a piece of fabric for the skirt; if necessary, sew fabric pieces together to obtain the width. Repeat for lining. Cut a piece of cording the same length as the long side of the fabric.

With edges aligned, sew the cording to the bottom edge of the right side of the skirt fabric. With the right sides together and the piping sandwiched between layers, sew the lining to the skirt fabric along the line of stitching at the bottom and on both sides, leaving the top edge open. Turn the skirt right side out; press.

Baste ¼ inch from the top edge. Cut monofilament to the finished skirt width. Tie each end to a T-pin and place the monofilament along the basting stitches. Zigzag-stitch over the monofilament ¼ inch from the top edge of the skirt, pulling the monofilament to gather the skirt while sewing.

Cut a 4-inch-wide fabric band to match the finished skirt width plus 3 inches. With the right sides together and cut edges aligned, center the band on the skirt top edge; sew together. Unfold and press the seams open. Press the ends of the band to the lining side of the skirt, even with the skirt edge. Turn under and press ½ inch along the unsewn edge of the band. Fold the band in half, enclosing the gathered edge of the skirt; press. With the skirt right side up, sew through all the layers ⅛ inch from the bottom edge of the band.

Attach the adhesive-backed side of the fastening tape to the inside edge of the sink. Sew the remaining half of the fastening tape to the front of the skirt band. Hang the skirt, beginning at the center and working toward the outer edges.

Resources

American Traditional Designs
800/448-6656
www.americantraditional.com

L. A. Stencilworks
877/989-0262
www.lastencil.com

Delta Technical Coatings
800/423-4135
www.deltacrafts.com

Hot Potatoes Fabric and Wall Stamps
615/269-8002
www.hotpotatoes.com

Plaid Enterprises
800/842-4197
www.plaidonline.com

Provo Craft
801/377-4311
www.provocraft.com

Royal Design Studio
800/747-9767
www.royaldesignstudio.com

Patterns

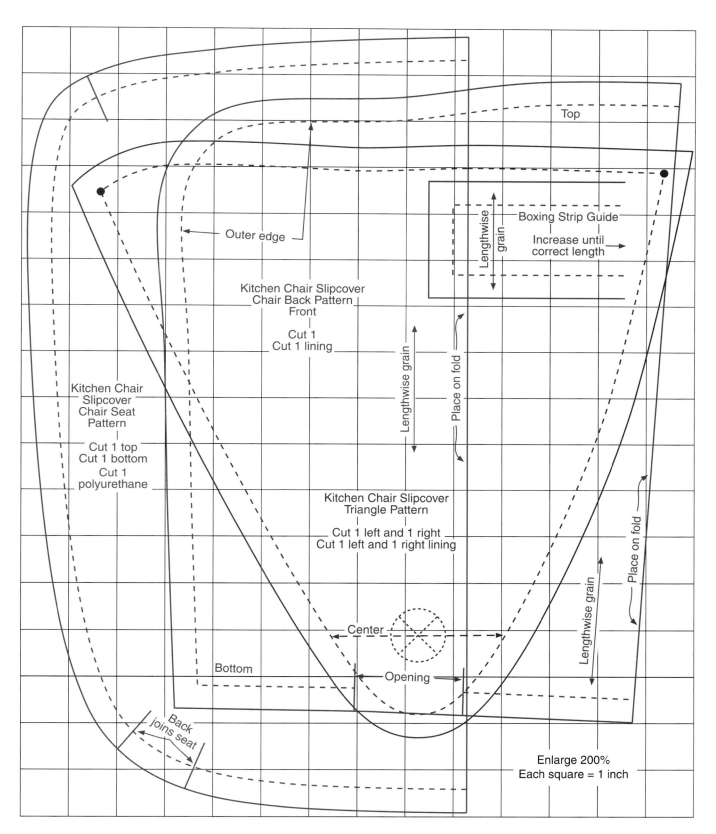

Top

Outer edge

Kitchen Chair Slipcover
Chair Back Pattern
Front

Cut 1
Cut 1 lining

Boxing Strip Guide

Increase until
correct length

Lengthwise grain

Kitchen Chair
Slipcover
Chair Seat
Pattern

Cut 1 top
Cut 1 bottom
Cut 1
polyurethane

Lengthwise grain

Place on fold

Kitchen Chair Slipcover
Triangle Pattern

Cut 1 left and 1 right
Cut 1 left and 1 right lining

Place on fold

Lengthwise grain

Center

Bottom

Opening

Back
joins seat

Enlarge 200%
Each square = 1 inch

Chair Cover Patterns *(page 98–99)*

Patterns

Enlarge 200%   Each square = 1 inch

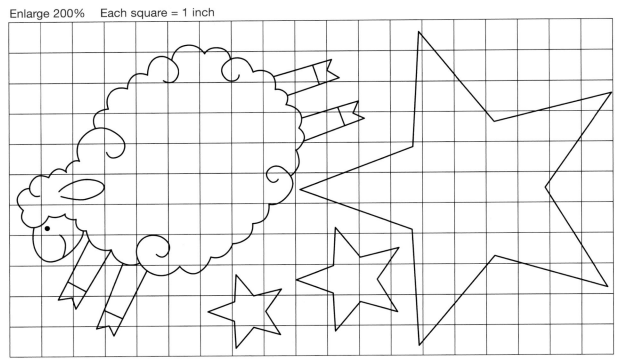

Lamb and Stars Pattern *(pages 118–123)*

Making a Bias Strip and Binding

Diagram 1

Diagram 2

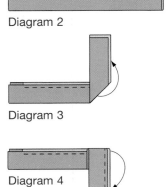

Diagram 3

Diagram 4

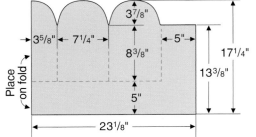

Bulletin Board - Diagram 1
(page 96)

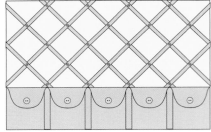

Bulletin Board - Diagram 2 *(page 96)*

Tufting Diagram *(page 102)*

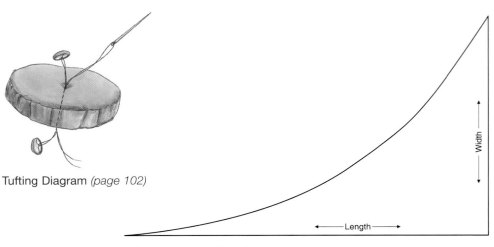

Table Runner Cutting Guide *(page 97)*